Latin Un
Translation

Latin Unseen Translation

Roy Hyde

Bristol Classical Press

This impression 2011
First published in 1998 by
Bristol Classical Press
an imprint of
Bloomsbury Academic
Bloomsbury Publishing Plc
36 Soho Square,
London W1D 3QY, UK
&
175 Fifth Avenue,
New York, NY 10010, USA

© 1998 by Roy Hyde

A catalogue record for this book is available
from the British Library

ISBN 978-1-85399-560-6

Printed and bound in Great Britain by
CPI Antony Rowe, Chippenham and Eastbourne

www.bloomsburyacademic.com

CONTENTS

PREFACE

The passages in this book are intended to provide material for practice in the unprepared translation of original Latin. The book was primarily designed for the use of students working towards U.K. A Level examinations, and to provide work for a two-year course, but it could just as well be used as part of a shorter course, and by students who have begun Latin at University.

The unseens are taken from authors commonly set in examinations at this level, though in the earlier part of the book I have used some extracts from Eutropius and from the *Ilias Latina* because of the relative accessibility of their Latin. I have adapted the original Latin only by making such omissions as have been necessary to condense narratives into passages of manageable length, and have not, except in a couple of minor instances, altered word-order in any way. I have tried to choose pieces of reasonable interest, though in the earlier part of the book I have paid more attention to finding straightforward Latin than to intrinsic interest.

The past twenty years have seen the production of a number of excellent introductory Latin courses, but no collection of passages intended for practice in the essential skill of unprepared translation of original Latin has appeared for more than a generation, and most of those still in use are much older, and contain much that is unusable by virtue of the length or difficulty of the extracts: I hope this book will go some way toward filling that gap.

I have incurred a number of debts while engaged on this project: John Betts of B.C.P. and I cooked up the original idea, and I owe thanks to him and Jean Scott and the rest of the B.C.P. staff for their patience; the Heads of the Classics Departments of the schools in the 'Eton Group' have seen and used some of the material, and encouraged me to persist; my colleagues at U.C.S., David Woodhead and Adrian McAra, have provided welcome advice and constructive criticism; and my own students have contributed much through their role as guinea-pigs. My two major debts, however, are to Robert West, Head of Classics at Bradford Grammar School, whose advice and encouragement and expertise have guided me from the beginning, and to my wife, Helen, whose word - processing skills have been absolutely indispensable, and who has encouraged me in every way to see the project through.

Finally: while this book has been in production I have had to mourn the dreadfully untimely deaths of two good friends; to the memory of my colleague Keith McCulloch and my student Ben Aird-Fairley this book, such as it is, is dedicated.

R.H., January 1998

ACKNOWLEDGEMENT: I am very grateful to John Dexter, Head of Classics at King's School, Peterborough, for his assistance in correcting a number of typographical errors for this reprint with amendments.

INTRODUCTION

GENERAL

This book consists of 150 passages of Latin, 75 prose and 75 verse. The first 50 passages, arranged according to author in groups of five, are shorter and for the most part easier, and could be used as the basis of a one year course in unseen translation. Within the groups of five, the passages are arranged in order of difficulty, and there is intended to be a rough gradient of difficulty throughout the first 50 pieces, though 'difficulty' is very much a subjective concept as far as unseen translation is concerned, and depends a good deal on the knowledge and experience of the individual student and on the type of Latin that he or she has met in other contexts. The order as it stands here is the order in which I, and my colleagues, have used the pieces: other teachers and other students may well prefer to follow different routes. I should not expect every unseen to be done as a written exercise: my usual practice is to select two or three from each group to be done in this way, and to do the rest as oral class exercises.

The remaining 100 passages are arranged in groups of 10, again according to author or genre. Numbers 51 to 130 are taken from authors regularly set in U.K. A Level examinations, or the equivalent, and users will probably wish either to select a variety of passages from the different groups, or concentrate for a time on one particular author. There should be sufficient material here to cover the second year of a two year course. I have not made any rigid attempt to grade the difficulty of passages within the groups, though in general the last one or two are somewhat longer and harder than the rest. The last 20 pieces are intended to more difficult, and equivalent to or harder than those normally set at S Level.

FORMAT OF THE UNSEENS

All the passages are arranged in the same way: a heading, in bold type, provides a summary or indication of what happens in the passage to be translated; following this is an English translation or paraphrase of the previous sentence or two of the original, printed in italics; then the Latin passage, in which words printed in bold type appear in the glossary below; finally, a glossary, divided into 'Words' and 'Names' (where the latter is appropriate), which translates or gives information about words and names which are not expected to be known: it should be noted that only such information is given as is required for a particular context, so that full principal parts of verbs, for example, will not necessarily be given, and that very familiar or regularly formed Latin names are not always glossed.

THE WORD LISTS

The Word Lists are an integral part of this book. Acquisition of vocabulary is a vital aspect of language learning, especially in Latin where word-order and syntax are often complex: a student with a wide knowledge of vocabulary can often make pretty good sense of even highly complex sentences without necessarily fully understanding the syntax, but one whose vocabulary knowledge is faulty will be floundering on two counts. Yet vocabulary learning, especially at this stage, is often done in a haphazard way, or left to the student's own inclination, or done in a hurry in the weeks immediately leading up to the examination. The Word Lists at the back of this book are an attempt to provide some structure to vocabulary learning, and to enable words to be learned, as far as possible, in some sort of context.

The Preliminary Word List contains c. 600 words which should be known before a student starts on the unseens. Reasons of space have made it impossible to provide a full vocabulary with meanings, but the majority of these words should be familiar to students who have followed one of the standard basic Latin courses up to the point where 'real' Latin is introduced (i.e. equivalent to G.C.S.E. standard in the U.K.), and the rest can easily be checked out and learned from one of the basic Latin dictionaries.

For the first 50 passages, each group of five has its own list of 40 words. These may be learned before the passages are attempted, or used for reference while the passages are being done and learned subsequently (though the sooner the better). It must be noted that these

Word Lists are cumulative: i.e. that when a word has appeared in a list it will not subsequently be glossed, unless it appears in an unusual sense; it is important therefore that if the teacher decides not to use, for example, any of the Caesar passages (nos. 11 - 15), the students nevertheless learn the words in Word List 3.

The same format is followed for the remaining 100 passages, except that here each group of 10 passages has a list of 50 words. and the lists are similarly cumulative. The lists as a whole, therefore, include a total of rather more that 1500 words which, though not intended to be exhaustive, should nevertheless amount to a working vocabulary sufficient to enable the student to tackle the average examination unseen with some degree of confidence.

1. The monarchy at Rome comes to an end when the last king's son rapes a noble woman and the royal family is driven out.

King Servius Tullius was murdered by his son-in-law Tarquinius Superbus, the son of the previous king, and his daughter, Tarquinius' wife.

L. Tarquinius Superbus, septimus atque ultimus regum, **Volscos**, quae gens non longe ab urbe est, vicit, **Gabios** et **Suessam Pometiam subegit**, cum **Tuscis** pacem fecit, et templum **Iovi** in **Capitolio** aedificavit. postea, **Ardeam** oppugnans, imperium perdidit. nam filius eius nobilissimam feminam Lucretiam, Collatini uxorem, **stupravit**, eaque, cum de iniuria marito et patri et amicis questa esset, in omnium conspectu se occidit. propter quam causam Brutus populum **concitavit** et Tarquinio ademit imperium. mox exercitus, qui civitatem **Ardeam** cum ipso rege oppugnabat, eum quoque reliquit; veniensque ad urbem rex, portis clausis, exclusus est, cumque **imperasset** annos quattuor et viginti cum uxore et liberis fugit.

Eutropius I.8

Words
subigo 3 **subegi subactum** = subdue; **stupro** 1 = rape; **concito** 1 = arouse; **imperasset** = **imperavisset** (n.b. **impero** here = rule)
Names
Volsci 2mpl = the Volsci (a people); **Gabii** 2mpl = Gabii (a place); **Suessa Pometia** 1f = Suessa Pometia (a place); **Tusci** 2mpl = the Etruscans (a people); **Iovi** is dat. of **Iuppiter** = the god Jupiter; **Capitolium** 2n = the Capitoline Hill in Rome; **Ardea** 1f = Ardea (a place).

1

2. The exile and triumphant return of Furius Camillus.

Twenty years after the capture and destruction of Fidenae, the men of Veii revolted; Furius Camillus, the Roman dictator, was sent against them and defeated them in battle. Soon afterwards he captured their city by siege.

cepit et **Faliscos**, non minus nobilem civitatem, sed commota est invidia quod praedam male divisisset, damnatusque ob eam causam et expulsus civitate est. statim **Galli** ad urbem venerunt et, victos Romanos apud flumen **Alliam** secuti, etiam urbem occupaverunt; neque defendi **quidquam** nisi **Capitolium** potuit. quod cum diu obsedissent et iam Romani fame **laborarent**, a Camillo, qui in vicina civitate **exsulabat, Gallis superventum est**, gravissimeque victi sunt. postea tamen, accepto auro ne **Capitolium** obsiderent, recesserunt; sed secutus eos Camillus ita **cecidit** ut et aurum quod his datum erat et omnia militaria signa quae ceperant **revocaret**. ita **tertio** triumphans urbem ingressus est et appellatus secundus Romulus, quasi et ipse patriae conditor.

Eutropius I.19

Words

quidquam = anything; **laboro** 1 (here) = be in trouble; **exsulo** 1 = be in exile; **Gallis superventum est** is an impersonal passive = "the Gauls were surprised"; **cecidit** is from **caedo**, not **cado**; **revoco** 1 (here) = get back; **tertio** = for a third time.

Names

Falisci 2mpl = Falerii (a place); **Gallus** 2m = a Gaul; **Allia** 1f = the river Allia; **Capitolium** 2n = the Capitoline Hill in Rome.

3. In the war between Pyrrhus of Epirus and the Romans, the two sides show their respect for each other.

At the same time, war was declared on the Tarentines, who live in the extreme south of Italy, because they had harmed some Roman envoys.

hi Pyrrhum, Epiri regem, contra Romanos **in auxilium** poposcerunt. is mox ad Italiam venit, tumque primum Romani cum **transmarino** hoste dimicaverunt. missus est contra eum consul P. Valerius Laevinus qui, cum exploratores Pyrrhi cepisset, iussit eos per castra duci, ostendi omnem exercitum, tumque dimitti ut renuntiarent Pyrrho quaecumque a Romanis agerentur. commissa mox pugna, Pyrrhus elephantorum auxilio vicit, sed nox proelio finem dedit; Laevinus tamen per noctem fugit, Pyrrhus Romanos mille octingentos cepit et eos summo honore tractavit, occisos sepelivit. quos cum **adverso vulnere** et **truci vultu** etiam mortuos iacere vidisset, tulisse ad caelum manus dicitur cum hac **voce**: se totius orbis dominum esse potuisse, si tales sibi milites **contigissent** .

Eutropius II.8

Words

in auxilium = for/to help; **transmarinus** adj = from across the sea; **adverso vulnere** = with wounds in the front of their bodies; **truci vultu** = with fierce expressions; **vox vocis** 3f (here) = word, remark; **contingo** 3 **contigi** (here) (+ dat) = belong to.

4. The defeated general Regulus refuses to persuade the Romans to make peace with Carthage and, feeling he is no longer a free man after being a prisoner of the Carthaginians, returns to Carthage to certain death.

In Sicily, Metellus the consul defeated a Carthaginian general, killing 20,000 men and capturing 26 elephants. He rounded up the fugitives and took them back to Rome with great ceremony.

post haec mala, **Carthaginienses** Regulum ducem, quem ceperant, rogaverunt ut Romam proficisceretur et pacem a Romanis obtineret et **permutationem** captivorum faceret. ille, Romam cum venisset, inductus in senatum dixit se, ex illa die qua in potestatem **Afrorum** venisset, Romanum esse desivisse. itaque senatui suasit ne pax cum **Poenis** fieret: illos enim, fractos tot casibus, spem nullam habere; se **tanti** non esse ut tot milia captivorum propter unum redderentur. itaque **obtinuit**. nam **Afros**, pacem petentes, nullus **admisit**. ipse **Carthaginem** rediit, offerentibusque Romanis ut eum Romae tenerent, negavit se in urbe mansurum in qua, postquam **Afris** servierat, dignitatem honesti civis habere non posset. regressus igitur ad Africam omnibus suppliciis exstinctus est.

Eutropius II.14

Words
permutatio permutationis 3f = exchange; **tanti** = worth so much; **obtinuit** = he got his wish; **admitto** 3 **admisi** (here) = listen to.
Names
Carthaginiensis Carthaginiensis 3m = Carthaginian; **Afer Afri** 2m = African; **Poenus** 2m = Carthaginian; **Carthago Carthaginis** 3f = Carthage.

5. The defeat of Pompey in the Civil War, and his treacherous murder in Egypt.

The consuls and senate, together with Pompey, fled to Greece and prepared for war there. Caesar entered the deserted city, and had himself elected dictator. Then he left for Spain and defeated three powerful armies of Pompey's supporters under Afranius, Petreius, and Varro.

inde regressus, in **Graeciam** transiit, **adversum** Pompeium dimicavit. primo proelio victus est et fugatus; evasit tamen quia, nocte **interveniente**, Pompeius sequi noluit; dixitque Caesar Pompeium nescire vincere, et **illo tantum die** se potuisse superari. deinde apud **Pharsalum**, productis utrimque ingentibus copiis, dimicaverunt. numquam **adhuc** Romanae copiae maiores **in unum** convenerant, totum terrarum orbem facile **subacturae**, si contra barbaros ducerentur. pugnatum est **ingenti contentione**, victusque **ad postremum** Pompeius, et castra eius **direpta** sunt. ipse fugatus **Alexandriam petiit** ut a rege **Aegypti** acciperet auxilia; qui, fortunam magis quam amicitiam secutus, occidit Pompeium; caput eius et **anulum** Caesari misit. quo conspecto, Caesar etiam lacrimas fudisse dicitur, tanti viri **intuens** caput, et **generi** quondam sui.

Eutropius VI.16

Words

adversum (+ acc) = against; **intervenio** 4 = intervene; **illo tantum die** = on that day only; **adhuc** (here) = up to that time; **in unum** = together/in one place; **subacturae** = capable of conquering; **ingenti contentione** = with tremendous passion; **ad postremum** = in the end; **diripio** 3 **diripui direptum** = plunder; **petiit** = **petivit**; **anulus** 2m = ring; **intueor** 2dep = look at; **gener generi** 2m = son-in-law (Pompey had formerly been married to Caesar's daughter).

Names

Graecia 1f = Greece; **Pharsalus** 2f = Pharsalus (a town in Greece); **Alexandria** 1f = Alexandria (a city in Egypt); **Aegyptus** 2f = Egypt.

5

6. The goddess Ceres, in disguise, is entertained by an old peasant couple and helps their sick child.

As the goddess accompanied him, the old man explained that his son was ill and could not sleep. Before entering the house, Ceres picked some sleep-inducing herbs and took them with her.

limen **ut** intravit, luctus videt omnia plena:
  iam spes in puero nulla salutis erat.
matre salutata (mater Metaneira vocatur),
  iungere **dignata est** os **puerile** suo.
pallor abit, **subitas**que vident in corpore vires:
  tantus caelesti venit ab ore vigor.
tota domus laeta est: hoc est materque paterque
  nataque; tres illi tota **fuere** domus.
Ovid, Fasti IV.537

Words

ut = when; **dignor** 1dep = deign, condescend; **puerilis** adj. = childish, of a child; **subitus** adj = sudden; **fuere** = **fuerunt**: a very common form, especially in verse.

7. **While the peasant couple sleep** (see previous passage) **Ceres tries to reward them by making their son immortal, but she is interrupted. As consolation, she says that he will be famous as the first agriculturalist.**

They put on a rustic feast in celebration. Ceres did not eat anything herself, but gave the boy some herbs mixed with warm milk to drink. Later, when all the others were asleep, she took him in her arms,

terque manu **permulsit** eum, tria carmina dixit,
  carmina mortali non **referenda sono**,
inque **foco**, corpus pueri vivente **favilla**
  obruit, humanum purget ut ignis onus.
excutitur somno stulte pia mater, et amens
  "quid facis?" exclamat, membraque ab igne rapit.
cui dea "**dum** non es," dixit, "scelerata, fuisti.
  irrita materno sunt mea dona metu.
iste quidem mortalis erit, sed primus arabit
  et seret et **culta** praemia tollet humo."

Ovid, Fasti IV.551

Words

ter = three times; **permulceo** 2 **permulsi** = stroke; **referendus** (gerundive of **refero**) = to be repeated; **sonus** 2m (here) = voice; **focus** 2m = hearth; **favilla** 1f = embers; **obruo** 3 **obrui** = cover; **humanus** adj (here) = of mortality; **purgo** 1 = purge, cleanse; **dum** (here) = although; **irritus** adj = vain, rendered useless; **maternus** adj = motherly; **iste** refers to the child; **cultus** adj = cultivated, grown.

8. Tarquinius Superbus wants to capture the town of Gabii: one of his three sons fools the Gabini into taking him in by claiming that he has been ill-treated by his father. (He will later betray the Gabini to Tarquinius.)

The last king of the Romans was Tarquinius, an unjust man, but a mighty warrior:

ceperat hic alias, alias **everterat** urbes,
   et **Gabios** turpi fecerat arte suos.
namque trium **minimus, proles manifesta** Superbi,
   in medios hostes, nocte silente, venit.
nudarant gladios: "occidite," dixit, "inermem!
   hoc **cupiant** fratres Tarquiniusque pater,
qui mea crudeli laceravit **verbere terga**."
   (dicere ut hoc posset, **verbera** passus erat.)
luna fuit: spectant iuvenes gladiosque **recondunt**,
   tergaque, deducta veste, **notata** vident.
Ovid, Fasti II.689

Words
everto 3 **everto** = destroy; **minimus** (here) = youngest; **proles prolis** 3f = offspring, son; **manifestus** adj = clear, true; **nudarant** = **nudaverant**: **nudo** 1 (here) = draw; **cupiant** = (they) would like...; **verber verberis** 3n = blow, lash; **terga** is plural with singular sense; **recondo** 3 = put away; **notatus** adj = marked.
Names
Gabii 2mpl = Gabii, a town near Rome.

9. When the god Saturn is deposed by his son Jupiter, the Giants produced by the Earth make war on him, but he defeats them.

For a long time, under the rule of Saturn, the gods of the Earth did not have to defer to the Sky gods, and the other heavenly bodies did not give way to Phoebus, but all the gods were honoured similarly.

hic **status** in caelo multos permansit **in** annos,
  dum senior fatis **excidit** arce deus.
Terra feros **partus**, immania monstra, **Gigantas**,
  edidit, **ausuros** in **Iovis** ire domum;
mille manus illis dedit et **pro** cruribus **angues**,
  atque ait **"in** magnos arma movete deos!"
exstruere hi montes ad sidera summa parabant
  et magnum bello sollicitare **Iovem**.
fulmina de caeli **iaculatus Iuppiter** arce
  vertit in auctores pondera vasta suos.

Ovid, Fasti V.33

Words

status 4m = state of affairs; **in** (here) = for; **dum** (here) = until; **excido** 3 **excidi** = fall from, be deposed from; **partus** 4m = offspring; **edo** 3 **edidi** = produce; **ausuros** = who would dare; **pro** (here) = instead of; **anguis anguis** 3c = snake; **in** (here) = against; **exstruo** 3 = build up, pile up; **iaculor** 1dep = hurl.

Names

Terra 1f = the goddess Earth; **Gigas Gigantis** 3m = Giant (**Gigantas** is acc pl); **Iuppiter** (acc **Iovem** gen **Iovis**) = the god Jupiter.

10. Chloris describes how the god Zephyrus carried her off, married her, and transformed her into Flora, goddess of Flowers.

I used to be called Chloris, and was a nymph of the countryside. Modesty forbids me to boast about my beauty, but it was enough to gain me a god for a husband.

ver erat, errabam: Zephyrus conspexit; abibam.
  insequitur, fugio; fortior ille fuit.
vim tamen **emendat** dando mihi **nomina nuptae**,
  inque meo non est ulla **querela toro**:
est mihi fecundus **dotalibus** hortus in agris;
  aura **fovet**, liquidae fonte **rigatur** aquae.
hunc meus implevit **generoso flore** maritus
  atque ait "**arbitrium** tu, dea, **floris** habe."
saepe ego **digestos** volui numerare colores,
  nec potui: numero copia maior erat.

              Ovid, Fasti V.201

Words

emendo 1 = make up for; **nomina** is plural with singular meaning; **nupta** 1f = bride; **querela** 1f = complaint; **torus** 2m = bed, marriage; **est mihi** = I have; **dotalis** adj = given (to me) as a wedding present; **foveo** 2 = warm; **rigatur** = (the garden) is watered by...; **generosus** adj (here) = beautiful; **flore** and **floris** are singular with plural meaning; **arbitrium** 2n (+ gen) = control over; **digesti** pl adj = various.

11. Caesar captures the Gallic town of Noviodunum after a short siege.

So, without any risk, our men went on killing the enemy as long as daylight permitted. They stopped at sunset and retreated into their camp, as they were ordered.

postridie Caesar, priusquam **se** hostes ex terrore ac fuga **reciperent**, in fines **Suessionum**, qui proximi **Remis** erant, exercitum duxit et, magno itinere confecto, ad oppidum Noviodunum contendit. id **ex itinere** oppugnare conatus, quod vacuum ab defensoribus esse audiebat, propter **latitudinem** fossae murique altitudinem, expugnare non potuit. castris munitis, **vineas agere** quaeque ad oppugnandum usui erant comparare coepit. interim omnis ex fuga **Suessionum** multitudo in oppidum proxima nocte convenit. celeriter **vineis** ad oppidum **actis**, **aggere iacto** turribusque constitutis, magnitudine operum, quae neque viderant ante Galli neque audierant, et celeritate Romanorum permoti, legatos ad Caesarem de deditione mittunt et, petentibus **Remis** ut conservarentur, impetrant.

Caesar, Gallic War II.12

Words

se...recipere (here) = to recover themselves; **ex itinere** = lit. straight from his march: "as soon as he got there"; **latitudo latitudinis** 3f = width; **vineas ago** 3 **egi actum** = to bring up protective sheds (to cover siege operations); **aggere iacto** = when a rampart had been constructed.

Names

Suessiones Suessionum 3mpl = the Suessiones; **Remi** 2mpl = the Remi (both Gallic tribes).

12. A battle for a hill between Caesar's men and those of Afranius and Petreius during the Civil War.

On the third day Caesar fortified a camp and ordered the rest of his cohorts, which he had left in previous camps, and his baggage, to be brought up to him.

erat inter oppidum **Ilerdam** et proximum collem, ubi castra Petreius atque Afranius habebant, **planities** circiter passuum CCC, atque in hoc fere medio spatio tumulus erat paulo **editior**; quem si occupavisset Caesar et communivisset, ab oppido et ponte et commeatu se **interclusurum adversarios** confidebat. hoc sperans, legiones III ex castris educit, **acie**que in locis idoneis instructa, unius legionis **antesignanos** procurrere atque eum tumulum occupare iubet. qua re cognita, celeriter **quae** in statione pro castris erant Afrani **cohortes** breviore itinere ad eum occupandum locum mittuntur. **contenditur proelio** et, quod prius in tumulum **Afraniani** venerant, nostri repelluntur atque, aliis **summissis** subsidiis, terga vertere seque ad signa legionum recipere coguntur.

Caesar, Civil War I.43

Words

planities 5f = a small plain; **editus** adj = high; **intercludo** 3 **interclusi interclusum** = cut off; **adversarius** 2m = enemy; **acies** 5f = battle-line; **antesignani** 2mpl = vanguard (lit. those who fight in front of the standards); **quae...cohortes** = the cohorts which...(the antecedent **cohortes** has been taken inside the relative clause); **contenditur proelio** = a battle took place; **summitto** 3 **submisi submissum** = send in.

Names

Ilerda 1f = Ilerda, a town; **Afraniani** 2mpl = Afranius' men.

13. Sabinus is treacherously murdered by Ambiorix, and his forces almost wiped out.

Sabinus ordered the tribunes and the senior centurions who were with him at the time to follow him. When they reached Ambiorix, he was told to lay down his arms. He did so, and ordered his men to do the same.

dum de condicionibus inter se **agunt**, longiorque **consulto** ab **Ambiorige** instituitur sermo, paulatim circumventus **interficitur**. tum vero, **more suo**, victoriam **conclamant** atque **ululatum** tollunt, impetuque in nostros facto, ordines perturbant. ibi **L.Cotta** pugnans interficitur cum maxima parte militum. reliqui se in castra recipiunt unde erant egressi. ex quibus **L.Petrosidius aquilifer**, cum magna multitudine hostium premeretur, **aquilam** intra vallum **proiecit**; ipse pro castris fortissime pugnans occiditur. illi aegre ad noctem **oppugnationem** sustinent: noctu **ad unum omnes**, desperata salute, se ipsi interfecerunt. pauci ex proelio elapsi incertis itineribus per silvas ad **T.Labienum** legatum in **hiberna** perveniunt atque eum de rebus gestis certiorem faciunt.

Caesar, Gallic War V.37

Words
ago de (+ abl) = talk about, discuss; **consulto** adv = deliberately; **interficitur**: the subject is Sabinus; **more suo** = in their usual way; **conclamo** 1 = acclaim; **ululatus** 4m = howling; **aquilam...proiecit**: Petrosidius does this so that the standard will not be captured by the enemy; **oppugnatio oppugnationis** 3f = attack; **ad unum omnes** = every single one of them; **hiberna** 2npl = winter camp.

Names
Ambiorix Ambiorigis 3m = Ambiorix, a Gallic chieftain; **L.Cotta** and **T.Labienus** are Roman officers, and **L.Petrosidius** a standard bearer (**aquilifer**).

14. During a chaotic attack on Gergovia, the centurion Petronius sacrifices himself to save his men.

Suddenly our allies the Aedui, whom Caesar had sent round by another route to cause a diversion, appeared on the right. Because their arms were the same as those of the other Gauls, our men did not recognise them as allies at first and were terrified.

eodem tempore L.Fabius centurio **quique** una murum ascenderant, circumventi atque interfecti, muro praecipitabantur. M.Petronius, eiusdem legionis centurio, cum portas **excidere** conatus esset, a multitudine oppressus ac sibi desperans, multis iam vulneribus acceptis, **manipularibus** suis qui illum secuti erant, "quoniam," inquit, "me una vobiscum servare non possum, vestrae certe vitae **prospiciam**, quos, cupiditate gloriae **adductus**, in periculum deduxi. vos, data facultate, vobis consulite." simul in medios hostes irrupit duobusque interfectis reliquos a porta paulum summovit. conantibus **auxiliari** suis, "frustra," inquit, "meae vitae subvenire conamini, quem iam sanguis viresque deficiunt. proinde abite, dum est facultas, vosque ad legionem recipite." ita pugnans post paulum concidit ac suis saluti fuit.

Caesar, Gallic War VII.50

Words

quique (qui+que) = and those who...; **excido** 3 = break down; **manipularis manipularis** 3m = fellow soldier; **prospicio** 3 (+ dat) = look out for, save; **adductus** adj = impelled, seduced; **auxilior** 1dep = help.

15. After routing the Germans, Caesar keeps some prisoners with him out of compassion.

The Germans were so surprised by our arrival that they could not decide whether to march out against us, defend their camp, or run away. Their panic was clear from their noise and running about, so our men, spurred on by remembering their treachery of the previous day, burst into the camp.

quo loco, qui celeriter arma capere potuerunt paulisper nostris restiterunt atque inter **carros** impedimentaque proelium commiserunt: at reliqua multitudo (nam cum omnibus suis domo excesserunt **Rhenum**que transierunt) passim fugere coepit; ad quos **consectandos** Caesar equitatum misit. Germani, post tergum clamore audito, cum suos interfici viderent, armis abiectis signisque militaribus relictis se ex castris eiecerunt; et cum ad **confluentem Mosae** et **Rheni** pervenissent, fuga desperata, magno numero interfecto, reliqui se in flumen praecipitaverunt atque ibi timore, **lassitudine**, vi fluminis perierunt. nostri **ad unum omnes** incolumes, perpaucis vulneratis, se in castra receperunt. Caesar eis quos in castris retinuerat discedendi **potestatem** fecit. illi, supplicia **cruciatus**que Gallorum veriti quorum agros vexaverant, remanere se apud eum velle dixerunt.

Caesar, Gallic War IV.14

Words

quo loco, qui = there, those who...; **carrus** 2m = wagon; **consector** 1dep = pursue; **confluens confluentis** 3m = confluence (place where rivers meet); **lassitudo lassitudinis** 3f = exhaustion; **ad unum omnes** = without exception; **potestas potestatis** 3f = opportunity; **cruciatus** 4m = torture.

Names

Rhenus 2m = the river Rhine; **Mosa** 1f = the river Meuse.

16. The Trojans, led by Hector, drive the Greeks back into their camp and on to their ships.

The Trojans pressed on: the Greeks fled into their camp, their strength exhausted, and strengthened their fortifications with strong barricades. But warlike Hector broke down the gates, splintering their timbers with a huge rock.

irrumpunt aditus **Phryges** atque in limine primo
restantes sternunt **Graecos** valloque **catervas**
deturbant; alii **scalas** in moenia ponunt
et iaciunt ignes: praebet victoria vires.
de muris pugnant **Danai** turresque per altas
saxa volant; subeunt, **acta testudine, Troes**
ascenduntque aditus et totis viribus instant.
turbati fugiunt omnes in castra **Pelasgi**
et **scandunt** puppes. urget **Troiana** iuventus
telaque crebra iacit: resonat clamoribus aether.

"Latin Iliad", 761

Words
caterva 1f = squadron, troop; **deturbo** 1 = dislodge; **scala** 1f = ladder; **acta testudine** = forming a "tortoise" (the military formation in which soldiers held their shields over their heads to form a protective "shell"); **scando** 3 (here) = get on board.

Names
Phryges Phrygum 3mpl = the Trojans; **Graeci 2mpl** = the Greeks; **Danai** 2mpl = the Greeks; **Troes Troum** 3mpl = the Trojans; **Pelasgi** 2mpl = the Greeks; **Troianus** adj = Trojan.

17. The gods intervene in the single combat between Aeneas and Diomedes, and Diomedes even manages to wound Venus.

Then Diomedes and Aeneas clashed together, first hurling their spears and then coming to close quarters. They hacked at each other with their swords: Diomedes could find no opportunity to inflict a serious wound with his sword:

saxum ingens, medio quod forte iacebat in agro,
sustulit et magno **conamine** misit in hostem.
ille ruit **prostratus** humi cum fortibus armis;
quem **Venus aethereas** genetrix delapsa per auras,
accipit et **nigra** corpus **caligine** texit.
non tulit **Oenides** animis nebulasque per ipsas
fertur et in **Venerem flagrantibus** inruit armis
caelestemque manum mortali vulnerat hasta.
icta petit caelum terris **Cytherea** relictis
atque ibi **sidereo queritur** sua vulnera **Marti**.

"Latin Iliad", 459

Words

sustulit: the subject is Diomedes; **conamen conaminis** 3n = effort; **prostratus** adj = prostrate, flat; **aethereus** adj = heavenly; **niger nigra nigrum** adj = black, dark; **caligo caliginis** 3f = cloud, mist; **fertur** = (he) hurled himself; **flagrans flagrantis** = blazing; **ictus** adj = (having been) struck; **sidereus** adj = heavenly; **queritur** = (she) complains about (+acc).

Names

Venus Veneris 3f = Venus; **Oenides Oenidis** 3m = Diomedes (descendant of Oeneus); **Cytherea** 1f = Venus; **Mars Martis** 3m = Mars.

18. Helen commiserates with her lover Paris on his defeat by her former husband Menelaus. Paris is still confident of success.

Menelaus hurled his great spear, but Venus snatched Paris away and carried him off to Helen's ornate chamber. Then she brought Helen to her lover. When she saw him, Helen said:

"venisti, mea **flamma**, **Paris**, superatus ab armis
coniugis antiqui? vidi, puduitque videre,
arreptum cum te traheret violentus **Atrides**
Iliacoque tuos **foedaret** pulvere crines.
quis tibi cum saevo **contendere** suasit **Atrida**?
an nondum **vaga** fama tuas pervenit ad aures
de virtute viri? moneo ne rursus **inique**
illius tua fata velis committere dextrae."
dixit, **dum largis perfudit fletibus ora**.
tristis **Alexander**, "non me superavit **Atrides**,
o meus ardor," ait, "sed castae **Palladis** ira.
mox illum nostris **succumbere** turpiter armis
aspicies, **aderit**que meo **Cytherea** labori."
                                                            "Latin Iliad", 319

Words

flamma 1f (here) = darling; **arripio** 3 **arripui arreptum** = seize; **foedo** 1 = defile; **contendo** 3 = fight; **an** = or; **vagus** adj = wandering, widespread; **inique** = on unequal terms; **dum largis...ora**: i.e. "while weeping bitterly"; **succumbo** 3 (+ dat) = succumb to, fall before; **aderit** (+ dat) = (she) will help...

Names

Paris Paridis 3m = Paris (also known as **Alexander Alexandri** 2m); **Atrides Atridis** 3m (abl **Atrida**) = Menelaus (son of Atreus); **Iliacus** adj = Trojan; **Pallas Palladis** 3f = the goddess Pallas Athene; **Cytherea** 1f = Venus.

18

19. Hector says farewell to his wife and baby son before going out to battle. His son, Astyanax, is frightened by Hector's plumed helmet.

When Hector realised that the Greeks were gaining ground, he ordered sacrifices to be made, and armed himself for war. Outside the walls, the battle continued to rage:

colloquium petit interea fidissima coniunx
Hectoris, **Andromache**, parvumque ad pectora natum
Astyanacta tenet; cuius dum maximus heros
oscula cara petit, subito perterritus infans
convertit timidos **materna** ad pectora vultus,
terribilemque fugit galeam **cristas**que **comantes**.
utque caput iuvenis **posito detexerat** aere,
protinus infantem geminis amplectitur **ulnis**,
attollensque manus, "precor, o pater optime," dixit,
"ut meus hic pro quo tua numina natus adoro
virtutes patrias primis imitetur ab annis."
                    "Latin Iliad", 563

Words
maternus adj = of (his) mother; **cristas...comantes** = the bristling plumes; **ut** (here) = when; **pono** 3 **posui positum** (here) = take off; **detego** 3 **detexi** = uncover; **ulna** 1f = arm; **ut...adoro** = "that my son here, on whose behalf I pray to your heavenly power..."
Names
Hector Hectoris 3m = Hector; **Andromache Andromaches** f = Andromache; **Astyanax Astyanactis** 3m (acc **Astyanacta**) = Astyanax.

20. King Priam of Troy begs Achilles to give up to him the body of his son Hector, whom Achilles has killed in battle.

Nothing could prevent Priam from going to Achilles and throwing himself on his mercy. The Greek leaders were amazed, and Achilles himself astounded, at the courage of the old man. Priam threw himself on his knees before Achilles, and raised his hands in supplication:

haec ait: "o **Graiae** gentis fortissime **Achilles**,
o regnis inimice meis, te **Dardana** solum
victa tremit **pubes**; te **sensit** nostra **senectus**
crudelem nimium: nunc **sis mitissimus**, oro,
donaque quae porto miseri pro corpore nati
accipias: si nec precibus nec flecteris auro,
in senis extremis **tua dextera saeviat** annis:
non vitam mihi nec magnos **concede** favores.
Hectoris interitu vicisti **Dardana** regna,
vicisti **Priamum**: sortis **reminiscere**, victor,
humanae, variosque ducum tu **respice** casus."
"Latin Iliad", 1027

Words

pubes pubis 3f = the young men; **sentio** 4 **sensi** (here) = recognise, regard; **senectus senectutis** 3f = the older men; **sis mitissimus...accipias** = "be merciful (and)...receive..."; **tua dextera saeviat...in** = "let your right hand commit its savagery on..."; **concedo** 3 = concede, yield; **interitus** 4m = death; **reminiscere** (imperative of **reminiscor** 3dep) (+ gen) = remember; **respicio** 3 (here) = reflect upon.

Names

Graius adj = Greek; **Achilles Achillis** 3m = Achilles; **Dardanus** adj = Trojan; **Hector Hectoris** 3m = Hector; **Priamus** 2m = Priam.

21. **The aged Hannibal, in exile, takes poison rather than fall into the hands of the Romans.**

The Senate sent envoys to request that King Prusias should surrender Hannibal to them. Prusias said that he would not do this himself, as it would be contrary to the laws of hospitality: but that they could try to capture him themselves if they wished, as they would easily find the place where he was living.

Hannibal enim uno loco se tenebat, in **castello** quod a rege datum erat, idque sic **aedificarat** ut in omnibus partibus aedificii exitus haberet, scilicet verens **ne usu veniret**, quod accidit. huc cum legati Romani venissent ac domum eius circumdedissent, puer, ab ianua prospiciens, **Hannibali** dixit plures armatos apparere. qui imperavit ei ut omnes fores aedificii circumiret ac propere sibi nuntiaret num eodem modo undique obsideretur. puer cum celeriter **quid esset** renuntiasset, omnesque exitus occupatos ostendisset, sensit id non **fortuito** factum, sed se peti neque sibi diutius vitam esse retinendam. **quam ne alieno arbitrio dimitteret**, memor pristinarum virtutum, venenum (quod semper secum habere **consuerat**) sumpsit.

Nepos, Hannibal 12

Words

castellum 2n = castle; **aedificarat** = **aedificaverat**; **ne usu veniret** = that this might turn out to be useful; **quid esset** = what the situation was; **fortuito** = by chance; **quam...dimitteret** = so as not to die at someone else's command; **consuerat** = **consueverat** (from **consuesco** 3 **consuevi**: am accustomed to).

Names

Hannibal Hannibalis 3m = Hannibal.

21

22. The Athenian commander Alcibiades, recalled from his post, fears that he will be punished. He flees to Sparta, where his strategy helps the Spartans in their war against Athens.

Just before the fleet sailed to Sicily, all the Hermae [small statues placed outside houses for good luck] in Athens were mutilated one night. It was rumoured that Alcibiades was involved. He wanted an investigation immediately, before the expedition, but his enemies thought it would be easier to make a case against him if he were not there: which is what they did.

nam postquam in **Siciliam** eum pervenisse crediderunt, **absentem**, **quod** sacra violasset, **reum fecerunt**. qua de re cum nuntius a magistratu missus esset ut domum ad causam dicendam rediret, in **trierem** quae ad eum erat deportandum missa ascendit. hac **Thurios** in Italiam pervectus, clam **se** ab custodibus **subduxit** et inde primum **Elidem**, dein **Thebas**, venit. postquam autem se **capitis damnatum**, bonis **publicatis**, audivit, **Lacedaemonem demigravit**. ibi, ut ipse **praedicare consuerat**, non adversus patriam sed inimicos bellum gessit, quod **eidem hostes essent civitati**. itaque huius consilio **Lacedaemonii** cum **Perse** rege amicitiam fecerunt, dein **Deceleam** in **Attica munierunt** praesidioque ibi perpetuo posito in obsidione **Athenas** tenuerunt. quo facto, multo superiores bello esse coeperunt.

Nepos, Alcibiades 4

Words

absens absentis adj = in (his) absence; **quod** + subj = on the grounds that; **reum facere** = to put [someone] on trial; **trieris trieris** 3f = trireme (a kind of ship); **se suducere subduxi** = sneak away; **capitis damno** 1 = condemn to death; **publico** 1 = confiscate; **demigro** 1 = move away; **praedico** 1 = say; **consuerat**: see note on previous passage; **eidem...civitati** = "enemies of the state were enemies of his"; **munierunt** = **muniverunt**.

Names

Sicilia 1f = Sicily; **Thurii** 2mpl = Thurii, a town in Italy; **Elis Elidis** 3f = Elis, a town in Greece; **Thebae** 1fpl = Thebes, a town in Greece; **Lacedaemon Lacedaemonis** 3f = Sparta; **Lacedaemonii** 2mpl = the Spartans; **Perses Persae** adj (abl **Perse**) = Persian; **Decelea** 1f = Decelea, a place in Attica (**Attica** 1f), near Athens (**Athenae** 1fpl).

23. With the Persian King's help, the Athenian admiral Conon organises a fleet to defeat Sparta and liberate Greece.

The King was impressed by Conon's personality, and undertook to help him prosecute the war against the Spartans. Pharnabazus was appointed by the King to organise the distribution of finances.

hinc, magnis muneribus donatus, ad mare est missus ut **Cypriis** et **Phoenicibus** ceterisque **maritimis** civitatibus **naves longas imperaret classem**que compararet. id ut **Lacedaemoniis** est nuntiatum, non sine cura rem **administrant**, quod maius bellum imminere arbitrabantur quam si cum barbaro rege solum **contenderent**. nam ducem fortem secum dimicaturum videbant, quem neque consilio neque copiis superare possent. **hac mente**, magnam contrahunt **classem**: proficiscuntur, **Pisandro** duce. hos **Conon** apud **Cnidum** adortus magno proelio fugat, multas naves capit, complures **deprimit**. qua victoria non solum **Athenae** sed etiam cuncta Graecia, quae sub **Lacedaemoniorum** fuerat imperio, liberata est. **Conon** cum parte navium in patriam venit, muros **dirutos** a **Lysandro** reficiendos **curat**, pecuniaeque quinquaginta talenta quae a **Pharnabazo** acceperat civibus suis donat.

Nepos, Conon 4

Words

maritimus adj = maritime, near the sea; **navis longa navis longae** f = warship; **impero** 1 (+ acc + dat) (here) = order (something) from (someone); **classis classis** 3f = fleet; **administro** 1 = manage, organise; **contendo** 3 = fight; **hac mente** = bearing this in mind; **deprimo** 3 (here) = sink; **diruo** 3 **dirui dirutum** = destroy; **curo** 1 + gerundive = get [something] done.

Names

Cyprii 2mpl = the Cypriots; **Phoenices Phoenicum** 3mpl = the Phoenicians; **Lacedaemonii** 2mpl = the Spartans; **Pisander Pisandri** 2m = Pisander, a Spartan commander; **Conon Cononis** 3m = Conon; **Cnidus** 2f = Cnidus, a town in Asia Minor; **Athenae** 1fpl = Athens; **Lysander Lysandri** 2m = Lysander, a Spartan commander; **Pharnabazus** 2m = Pharnabazus.

24. In a letter, Themistocles, exiled from Greece, offers his services to Artaxerxes, the son of his former enemy King Xerxes of Persia, with the promise of a plan that will help Artaxerxes' cause.

I know [Nepos writes] that many authors say that Themistocles went to Persia while Xerxes was still King. But I am more inclined to believe Thucydides, who lived not long after these events. He says that it was Artaxerxes that he approached, and sent him the following letter:

"Themistocles veni ad te, qui plurima mala omnium **Graiorum** in domum tuam **intuli, quamdiu** mihi necesse fuit **adversum** patrem tuum bellare patriamque meam defendere. **idem** multo plura bona feci, postquam ego ipse **in tuto** et **ille** in periculo esse coepit. nam cum in **Asiam** reverti vellet, proelio apud **Salamina** facto, litteris eum certiorem feci **id agi** ut pons quem in **Hellesponto** fecerat dissolveretur: quo nuntio periculo est liberatus. nunc autem confugi ad te, **exagitatus** a cuncta Graecia, tuam petens amicitiam: quam si ero adeptus, non minus me bonum amicum habebis quam fortem inimicum ille expertus est. te autem rogo ut, de iis rebus quas tecum **colloqui** volo, **annuum** mihi **tempus** des, **eo**que **transacto ad te venirem patiaris.**"

Nepos, Themistocles 9

Words
infero inferre intuli = inflict; **quamdiu** = as long as; **adversum** (+ acc) = against; **idem** = I, that same man...; **in tuto** = safe; **ille**: i.e. Xerxes; **id agi** = "[that] action was being taken..."; **exagito** 1 = drive out; **colloquor** 3dep = have talks; **annuum...tempus** = a period of a year; **eo...transacto** = when that is over; **ad...patiaris**: the object of **patiaris** is "me" - more normal syntax would be **me patiaris ut ad te venirem.**
Names
Graius 2m = Greek; **Asia** 1f = Asia Minor; **Salamis Salaminos** f = the island of Salamis; **Hellespontus** 2m = the Hellespont (the strait that separates Asia Minor from Europe).

25. Atticus and one of his friends are unexpectedly saved by Antony's respect for him.

Then there was a sudden change of fortune. Antony returned to Italy, and everyone thought that Atticus would be in serious danger because of his close friendship with Cicero and Brutus.

itaque **ad** adventum **imperatorum de foro decesserat**, timens **proscriptionem**, latebatque apud P.Volumnium, cui paulo ante opem tulerat (tanta **varietas** iis temporibus fuit fortunae ut **modo** hi **modo** illi in summo essent aut **fastigio** aut periculo), habebatque secum Q.Gellium Canum, aequalem simillimumque sui. Antonius autem, etsi **tanto odio ferebatur in Ciceronem** ut non solum ei sed etiam omnibus eius amicis esset inimicus, eosque vellet **proscribere**, multis hortantibus, tamen Attici memor fuit officii, et ei, cum **requisisset** ubi esset, sua manu scripsit ne timeret statimque ad se veniret: se eum et, illius causa, Canum de **proscriptorum** numero **exemisse**. ac ne quod periculum incideret, praesidium ei misit. sic Atticus, in summo **timore**, non solum sibi sed etiam ei quem carissimum habebat, praesidio fuit.

Nepos, Atticus 10

Words

ad (here) (+ acc) = at; **imperatores** = the triumvirs, Antony, Octavian and Lepidus; **de foro decedo** 3 **decessi** = leave public life; **proscriptio proscriptionis** 3f = proscription (a process by which the triumvirs eliminated their political enemies by declaring them outlaws); **varietas varietatis** 3f = changeability; **modo...modo** = sometimes...sometimes...; **fastigium** 2n = rank, status; **tanto odio ferebatur in** = "he was so implacably hostile to..."; **proscribo** 3 = proscribe, outlaw; **requiro** 3 **requisi** = find out; **proscripti** 2mpl = proscribed men, outlaws; **eximo** 3 **exemi** = take out, remove; **timor timoris** 3m (here) = crisis.

Names

Cicero Ciceronis 3m = Cicero.

26. Ovid contrasts his fate as an exile with the wanderings of Ulysses.

You poets ought to write about my troubles, not Ulysses', because I've put up with more than he did. He travelled around in a small area over a long period of time: I've crossed seas that are constellations apart since Caesar's anger exiled me to the land of the Getae.

ille habuit fidamque **manum** sociosque fideles:
  me **profugum** comites deseruere mei.
ille suam laetus patriam victorque petebat:
  a patria fugi victus et exsul ego.
illi corpus erat durum **patiens**que laborum:
  invalidae vires **ingenua**eque mihi.
ille **erat assidue** saevis **agitatus in** armis:
  assuetus studiis mollibus ipse fui.
me deus oppressit, nullo mala nostra **levante**;
  bellatrix illi **diva** ferebat opem.

                    Ovid, Tristia I.5.63

Words
ille = Ulysses; **manus** 4f (here) = band of men; **profugus** 2m = fugitive; **patiens patientis** adj (+gen) = capable of bearing; **ingenuus** (here) = feeble; **erat assidue agitatus in** = he had been continually involved in...; **levo** 1 = alleviate; **bellatrix...diva**: the "warrior goddess" was Athene, who watched over Ulysses.

27. Ovid describes the moment when he had to leave his home and go into exile, and how his wife wanted to go with him.

"I will embrace you while I can: I may never be able to again, so I count every moment with you as precious..." I could say no more; inconsolably I embraced all those most dear to me.

dum loquor et flemus, caelo nitidissimus alto,
    stella gravis nobis, **Lucifer**, ortus erat.
dividor **haud aliter quam si** mea membra relinquam,
    et pars **abrumpi** corpore visa suo est.
tum vero exoritur clamor gemitusque **meorum**,
    et feriunt maestae pectora nuda manus.
tum vero coniunx, umeris **abeuntis** inhaerens,
    miscuit haec lacrimis tristia verba meis:
"non potes avelli! simul hinc, simul ibimus!" inquit;
    "te sequar et coniunx exsulis exsul ero.
te iubet e patria discedere Caesaris ira,
    me pietas: pietas haec mihi Caesar erit."
Ovid, Tristia I.3.71

Words
haud aliter quam si = just as if; **abrumpi** (+ abl) = "to be torn away from"; **mei** 2mpl = my family; **abeuntis** = (lit) = "of me as I went away".

Names
Lucifer Luciferi 2m = the Morning Star.

28. Ovid complains that the hardships of his life in exile make him look even older than he is.

Now I am becoming old and grey, wrinkles furrow my face, and the energy and vigour are deserting my broken body.

nec, si me subito videas, agnoscere possis:
  aetatis facta est tanta **ruina** meae.
confiteor facere hoc annos, sed et altera causa est:
  anxietas animi, continuusque labor.
nam mea per longos si quis mala digerat annos,
  crede mihi, **Pylio Nestore maior** ero.
cernis **ut**, in duris (et quid bove firmius?) arvis,
  fortia taurorum corpora frangat opus:
me quoque **debilitat series** immensa malorum,
  ante meum tempus cogit **et** esse senem.
otia corpus alunt; animus quoque pascitur **illis**:
  immodicus contra carpit utrumque labor.

Ovid, Letters from Pontus I.4.5

Words

aetas aetatis 3f (here) = life; **ruina** 1f = ruin; **nam...annos** = "for if you distribute my sufferings evenly over a period of years": together with the next line, Ovid is saying that he has had enough sufferings to last the longest possible lifetime; **maior maioris** adj (here) = older; **ut** (here) = how; **debilito** 1 = wear out; **series seriei** 5f = series; **et** needs to be translated at the beginning of the line; **otia** is plural with singular meaning, and is referred to by **illis**; **immodicus** adj = excessive; **contra** (here) = on the contrary; **carpo** 3 (here) = weaken; **utrumque** = each of them (i.e. both mind and body).

Names

Nestor Nestoris 3m = Nestor, King of Pylos (**Pylius** adj), who was legendary for his great age.

29. Ovid complains of the problems of being ill at Tomis; the thought of his wife is the only thing that makes him feel better.

If you're wondering why this letter is written by someone else's hand, it's because I've been ill.

aeger in extremis ignoti partibus orbis,
  incertusque meae paene salutis eram.
nec caelum patior, nec aquis assuevimus istis,
  terraque nescioquo non placet ipsa modo.
non domus **apta** satis, non hic cibus utilis aegro,
  nullus **Apollinea** qui **levet arte** malum.
lassus in extremis iaceo populisque locisque,
  et **subit affecto** nunc **mihi** quidquid abest.
omnia **cum** subeant, vincis tamen omnia, coniunx,
  et **plus in nostro pectore parte tenes**.
te loquor absentem, te vox mea **nominat** unam;
  nulla venit sine te nox mihi, nulla dies.
                              Ovid, Tristia III.3.2

Words
incertus adj = unsure; **nec caelum patior** = I can't bear the climate; **aptus** adj = suitable; **levo** 1 = alleviate; **subit affecto...mihi** ="there comes into my mind, in my affliction..."; **cum** (here) = although; **plus...tenes** = "you have the greatest part of my affection"; **nomino** 1 = name, call upon.

Names
Apollinea ars Apollineae artis f = the art of Apollo (i.e. medicine, of which Apollo was the god).

29

30. Barbarous invaders raid Tomis in the winter, murdering, plundering and enslaving the inhabitants, and making agriculture futile.

So when the bitter North Wind has frozen over the sea and the rivers, murderous barbarians descend on us on their fast horses and lay waste the countryside round about.

diffugiunt alii, nullisque **tuentibus** agros
 incustoditae **diripiuntur opes**:
ruris **opes** parvae, pecus et **stridentia** plaustra,
 et quas divitias incola pauper habet.
pars agitur vinctis post tergum capta lacertis,
 respiciens frustra rura laremque suum:
pars cadit **hamatis** misere **confixa** sagittis,
 nam **volucri** ferro **tinctile virus** inest.
quae nequeunt secum ferre aut abducere, perdunt,
 et **cremat insontes** hostica flamma casas.
tunc quoque, cum pax est, trepidant formidine belli,
 nec quisquam, **presso vomere**, **sulcat** humum.
Ovid, Tristia III.10.57

Words

tueor 2dep = protect; **diripio** 3 = plunder; **opes opum** 3fpl = property; **strideo** 2 = creak; **pars...pars** = some...others; **hamatus** adj = barbed; **configo** 3 **confixi confixum** = pierce; **volucris** adj = flying; **tinctile virus** = poison; **cremo** 1 = burn down; **insons insontis** adj = innocent; **presso vomere** = "working the ploughshare"; **sulco** 1 = plough.

31. After usurping the Kingdom of Numidia and murdering the brother of King Adherbal, Jugurtha resorts to bribery to try to avert Roman intervention.

The Numidians were divided: Adherbal had more support, but Jugurtha's followers included the more warlike elements. So Jugurtha assembled as large an army as possible, and either by force or voluntarily began to attach the cities of Numidia to his cause, in an attempt to take over the whole kingdom.

Adherbal, tametsi Romam legatos miserat qui senatum **docerent** de caede fratris, tamen fretus multitudine militum parabat **armis contendere**. sed ubi res ad certamen venit, victus ex proelio fugit in **provinciam** ac deinde Romam contendit. tum Iugurtha **timere** populum Romanum, neque adversus iram **eius** usquam nisi in avaritia **nobilitatis** et pecunia sua spem **habere**. itaque paucis diebus cum auro et argento multo Romam legatos mittit, quibus praecipit primum ut veteres amicos muneribus **expleant**, deinde novos **acquirant**, postremo quaecumque possint **largiendo** parare ne cunctarentur. sed ubi Romam legati venere et **ex praecepto** regis **hospitibus** aliisque, **quorum ea tempestate in senatu auctoritas pollebat**, magna munera misere, **tanta commutatio incessit** ut ex maxima invidia in gratiam **nobilitatis** Iugurtha veniret.

Sallust, Jugurtha 13

Words

doceo 2 (here) = tell; **armis contendo** 3 = go to war; **provincia** 1f = the Roman province in North Africa; ·**timere** and **habere** are historic infinitives: translate as imperfects, with Jugurtha as the subject; **eius** = its: i.e. "of the Roman people"; **nobilitas nobilitatis** 3f (here) = the (Roman) noblemen; **expleo** 2 (here) = satisfy; **acquiro** 3 = acquire; **largiendo** = by giving out money; **ex praecepto** = according to the command; **hospitibus**: i.e. Jugurtha's friends in Rome; **quorum...pollebat** = "who were most influential in the senate at that time"; **tanta...incessit** = "such a change of heart took place".

31

32. Jugurtha makes ever more vehement efforts to provoke the peaceable Adherbal into war.

Having gained part of the kingdom by bribing the Romans, and being convinced that anything could be achieved at Rome by money, Jugurtha set his heart on Adherbal's territory. Jugurtha was fierce and warlike; the man he attacked was peaceable, unwarlike, gentle, and open to attack - more fearful than fearsome.

igitur **ex improviso** fines eius cum magna **manu** invadit, multos mortales capit, aedificia incendit, pleraque loca hostiliter cum equitatu **accedit**, deinde cum omni multitudine in regnum suum convertit, existimans **Adherbalem**, iniurias suas **manu vindicaturum**, eamque rem belli causam **fore**. at ille, quod neque se parem armis existimabat, et amicitia populi Romani magis quam **Numidis** fretus erat, legatos ad Iugurtham de iniuriis **questum** misit. qui tametsi **contumeliosa** dicta rettulerant, **prius** tamen omnia pati decrevit **quam** bellum sumere. neque **cupido** Iugurthae **minuebatur**. itaque non, ut antea, cum **praedatoria manu**, sed magno exercitu bellum gerere coepit et aperte totius **Numidiae** imperium petere. ceterum **qua pergebat**, urbes agros **vastare**, praedas **agere**, hostibus terrorem **augere**.

Sallust, Jugurtha 20

Words

ex improviso = unexpectedly; **manus** 4f (here) = band of men; **accedo** 3 (here) = attack; **manu** = by armed force; **vindico** 1 = avenge; **fore**: future infinitive of **esse**; **questum** (supine of purpose) = "to complain"; **contumeliosus** adj = insulting; **prius...quam** is equivalent to **priusquam**; translate in the place in the sentence where **quam** occurs; **cupido cupidinis** 3m = greed; **minuo** 3 = diminish; **praedatoria manus** f = raiding party; **qua** = wherever; **pergo** 3 = go; **vastare**, **agere**, and **augere** are historic infinitives: see note on previous passage.

Names

Adherbal Adherbalis 3m = Adherbal; **Numida** 1m = Numidian; **Numidia** 1f = Numidia.

33. **Despite his fear of the Romans, Jugurtha's greed impels him to try to capture the town of Cirta; diplomatic activity fails to stop him.**

Several distinguished elder statesmen were sent to Africa, incuding M.Scaurus, an ex-consul and at that time the senior member of the Senate. When they arrived they immediately communicated with Jugurtha and told him to come to the province without delay.

ille ubi **accepit** homines claros, **quorum auctoritatem Romae pollere audiverat**, contra **inceptum** suum venisse, primo, commotus metu atque libidine, **diversus agitabatur**. timebat iram senatus, ni paruisset legatis: porro animus, **cupidine** caecus, **ad inceptum scelus rapiebatur**. vicit tamen in avido ingenio pravum consilium. igitur summa vi Cirtam irrumpere **nititur**, maxime sperans aut vi aut dolis **sese** casum victoriae inventurum. quod ubi **secus procedit** neque quod intenderat efficere potest, ne **amplius** Scaurum, quem plurimum metuebat, incenderet, cum paucis equitibus in **provinciam** venit. ac tametsi graves **minae** nuntiabantur quod ab oppugnatione non desisteret, multa tamen oratione consumpta legati frustra discessere.

Sallust, Jugurtha 25

Words

accipio 3 **accepi** (here) = find out; **quorum...audiverat** = "whom he had heard were highly influential at Rome"; **inceptum** 2n = enterprise; **diversus agitabatur** = he was caught in two minds; **cupido cupidinis** 3m = greed; **ad...rapiebatur** = "was drawn towards the criminal course he had embarked upon"; **nitor** 3dep = strive; **sese** = **se**; **secus procedit** = (it) went badly; **amplius** = any more; **provincia** 1f = the Roman province in North Africa; **minae** 1fpl = threats.

33

34. Catilina's plot against Cicero is foiled by the spy Curius.

Catilina had sent Manlius to Etruria, and others to other places that he thought would be useful to his plot. Meanwhile he was busy at Rome with various schemes. He was always armed and ready at all times, and he ordered his men to be the same; he was constantly vigilant, and always on the move.

postremo, ubi **nihil procedit**, rursus **intempesta nocte** coniurationis principes convocat **per** M.Porcium Laecam, ibique, multa de ignavia eorum questus, **docet** se Manlium praemisisse ad eam multitudinem quam paraverat, **item** alios in alia loca opportuna, qui initium belli facerent, **seque** ad exercitum proficisci cupere, si prius **Ciceronem** oppressisset. igitur, perterritis ac dubitantibus ceteris, C. Cornelius, eques Romanus, **operam** suam **pollicitus**, et cum eo L.Vargunteius senator. constituere ea nocte paulo post cum armatis hominibus sicuti **salutatum introire** ad **Ciceronem** ac domi suae imparatum **confodere**. Curius, ubi intellegit quantum periculum consuli **impendeat**, **propere Ciceroni** dolum qui parabatur enuntiat. ita illi, ianua prohibiti, tantum facinus frustra susceperant.

Sallust, Catilina 27

Words

nihil procedit = no progress was made; **intempesta nocte** = at the dead of night; **per** is equivalent to **apud**; **docet** = he told them; **item** = in the same way; **seque** = "and that he (himself)..."; **opera** 1f = help; **pollicitus** = **pollicitus est**; **salutatum** = to pay their respects to him; **introeo introire** = go in; **confodio** 3 = stab to death; **impendeo** (+ dat) = threaten; **propere** adv = quickly.

Names

Cicero Ciceronis 3m = Cicero.

34

35. Petreius defeats Catilina, despite fierce resistance from both Catilina and his men.

When he had made sure of everything, Petreius gave the signal to advance, ordering his cohorts to move forward steadily. The enemy did the same. Soon they were close enough for the light-armed soldiers to engage:

maximo clamore cum infestis signis concurrunt; pila **omittunt**, gladiis res geritur; veterani, pristinae virtutis memores, comminus acriter **instare**; illi haud timidi resistunt; maxima vi **certatur**. interea Catilina cum **expeditis** in prima acie **versari**, **laborantibus** succurrere, omnia providere, multum ipse pugnare, saepe hostem ferire; **strenui** militis et boni imperatoris **officia** simul **exsequebatur**. Petreius, ubi videt Catilinam, **contra ac ratus erat**, magna vi **tendere**, **cohortem praetoriam** in medios hostes inducit, eosque perturbatos atque alios resistentes interfecit. deinde ex lateribus ceteros aggreditur. Catilina, postquam fusas copias seque cum paucis relictum videt, memor generis atque pristinae suae dignitatis, in **confertissimos** hostes incurrit ibique pugnans **confoditur**.

Sallust, Catilina 50

Words

omitto 3 (here) = throw; **instare** is historic infinitive; **certatur** = they fought; **expediti** 2mpl = light-armed soldiers; **versor** 1dep = am engaged (**versari** is historic infinitive, as are the other infinitives in this sentence); **laboro** 1 (here) = be in difficulties; **strenuus** (here) = brave; **officia...exsequebatur** = he performed the duties...; **contra...erat** = contrary to what he had expected; **tendo** 3 (here) = fight; **cohors praetoria** = the praetorian cohort (the soldiers commanded by the general in person); **confertissimos** = "where they were most densely packed"; **confodio** 3 = stab to death.

36. As Cadmus is turned into a snake, his wife prays to be transformed as well.

Cadmus wanted to say more, but suddenly his tongue was split into two, and as he tried to speak, all he could do was hiss.

nuda manu feriens exclamat pectora coniunx,
"Cadme, quid hoc? ubi pes? ubi sunt umerique, manusque?
et color, et facies et, dum loquor, omnia? cur non
me quoque, **caelestes**, in **eandem** vertitis anguem?"
dixerat: ille suae **lambebat** coniugis ora
inque sinus caros, veluti cognosceret, ibat,
et dabat amplexus assuetaque colla petebat.
quisquis adest (aderant comites) terretur; at illa
lubrica permulcet **cristati** colla draconis,
et subito duo sunt **iunctoque volumine** serpunt,
donec in **appositi** nemoris subiere latebras.

Ovid, Metamorphoses IV.591

Words

caelestes 3mpl = gods; **eandem** (here) = the same kind of; **lambo** 3 = lick; **lubricus** adj = smooth; **cristatus** adj = crested; **iuncto...volumine** = with their coils entwined; **appositus** adj = nearby.

37. Coronis explains why and how she was turned into a bird.

I was walking slowly along the shore as usual, when the god of the sea saw me and desired me. When he found that he couldn't seduce me with words, he turned to force and tried to grab me:

> fugio, densumque relinquo
> litus, et in molli nequiquam **lassor** harena.
> inde deos hominesque voco, nec **contigit** ullum
> vox mea mortalem; mota est pro virgine **Virgo**,
> auxiliumque tulit. tendebam bracchia caelo:
> bracchia coeperunt levibus **nigrescere** pennis;
> **plangere** nuda meis conabar pectora palmis,
> sed neque iam palmas nec pectora nuda **gerebam**;
> currebam nec, ut ante, pedes retinebat harena,
> sed summa tollebar humo; mox, acta per auras,
> evehor et data sum comes **inculpata Minervae**.

Ovid, Metamorphoses II.576

Words
lassor 1dep = exhaust oneself; **contingo** 3 **contigi** (here) = reach;
nigresco 3 = become dark; **plango** 3 = beat; **gero** 3 (here) = have;
inculpatus adj = blameless, chaste.

Names
Virgo Virginis 3f = the Virgin Goddess (= **Minerva** 1f).

37

38. Io has been changed into a cow. Accompanied by Argus, who keeps watch over her, she comes to her father, the river-god Inachus, but cannot communicate with him.

Even when she wanted to hold out her arms in supplication to Argus, she could not, because she had no arms now, and when she tried to complain she could only moo, and was terrified of the sound of her own voice.

venit et ad ripas ubi ludere saepe solebat,
Inachidas ripas, novaque ut conspexit in unda
cornua, pertimuit, seque **exsternata** refugit.
Naides ignorant, ignorat et **Inachus** ipse
quae sit. at illa patrem sequitur sequiturque sorores,
et patitur tangi seque **admirantibus** offert.
decerptas senior porrexerat **Inachus** herbas:
illa manus **lambit** patriisque dat oscula palmis
nec retinet lacrimas; et si modo verba sequantur,
oret opem nomenque suum casusque loquatur.

Ovid, Metamorphoses I.639

Words

exsternatus adj = terrified; **admirantibus** = "for their admiration"; **decerpo** 3 **decerpsi decerptum** = pluck; **senior** = **senex**; **lambo** 3 = lick.

Names

Inachis Inachidos f adj (acc pl **Inachidas**) = belonging to the river-god **Inachus** (2m); **Naides Naidum** 3fpl = nymphs.

39. Narcissus sees his reflection in a pool and falls in love with it.

Here, exhausted by hunting in the heat of the day, Narcissus lay down,
attracted by the appearance of the place and by the cool water;

dumque sitim **sedare** cupit, sitis altera crevit,
dumque bibit, visae **correptus** imagine formae,
spem sine corpore amat: corpus putat esse, quod unda est.
adstupet ipse sibi, vultuque immotus eodem
haeret ut e **Pario formatum** marmore **signum**.
se cupit imprudens et, qui probat, ipse probatur,
dumque petit petitur, pariterque accendit et ardet.
irrita fallaci quotiens dedit oscula fonti!
in mediis quotiens visum **captantia** collum
bracchia mersit aquis, nec se **deprendit** in illis!
Ovid, Metamorphoses III.415

Words
sedo 1 = quench; **corripio** 3 **corripui correptum** (here) = captivate;
formo 1 = make, sculpt; **signum** 2n (here) = statue; **irritus** adj = vain;
fallax fallacis adj = deceptive; **captantia** (npl, agreeing with **bracchia**)
= trying to embrace; **deprendo** 3 **deprendi** = catch, get hold of.
Names
Parius adj = from Paros, an island famous for its marble.

40. Phaethon, who has been allowed by the Sun-god to drive the horses of the sun (to show that he really is the god's son), realises that they are out of control.

He was terrified and did not know which way to turn the reins, and if he had known he would not have been able to do it.

ut vero summo despexit ab aethere terras
infelix Phaethon **penitus penitusque** iacentes,
palluit et subito genua **intremuere** timore,
et iam mallet equos numquam tetigisse **paternos**.
iam **cognosse** genus piget et **valuisse rogando**.
quid faciat? multum caeli post terga relictum,
ante oculos plus est. animo **metitur** utrumque;
et **modo**, quos illi fatum **contingere** non est,
prospicit occasus, **interdum** respicit ortus,
quidque agat ignarus, stupet et nec **frena remittit**
nec retinere valet nec nomina novit equorum.

Ovid, Metamorphoses II.178

Words

penitus penitusque = far, far below; **pallesco** 3 **pallui** = go pale; **intremisco** 3 **intremui** = start to tremble; **paternus** adj = of (his) father; **cognosse** = **cognovisse**: "to have tried to find out"; **valuisse rogando** = "to have got his wish" (i.e. to drive the horses of the sun); **metior** 4dep = calculate,measure ; **modo...interdum**; sometimes...sometimes; **contingo** 3 = reach; **frena** 2npl = reins; **remitto** 3 = let go of.

41. The cowardly admiral Cleomenes abandons his fleet to attack by pirates.

If Cleomenes had not fled, the others would have had some hope of resistance, but he made off towards Helorus, and the rest followed, not so much fleeing from the pirates as trying to catch up with their admiral. And so the pirates were able to pick them off one at a time.

ita prima **Haluntinorum** navis capitur, cui praeerat **Haluntinus** homo nobilis, Phylarchus, quem ab illis praedonibus **Locrenses** postea **publice redemerunt.** deinde **Apolloniensis** navis capitur, et eius praefectus Anthropinus occiditur. haec dum aguntur, interea **Cleomenes** iam ad **Helori** litus pervenerat; iam sese in terram e navi eiecerat **quadriremem**que **fluctuantem** in **salo** reliquerat. reliqui praefecti navium, cum in terram imperator exisset, cum ipsi neque repugnare neque mari effugere ullo modo possent, **appulsis** ad **Helorum** navibus **Cleomenem** persecuti sunt. tum praedonum dux, **Heracleo**, repente praeter spem non sua virtute sed **istius** avaritia nequitiaque victor, classem pulcherrimam populi Romani, in litus eiectam, cum primum **invesperasceret**, inflammari incendique iussit.

Cicero, Against Verres II.5.90

Words

publice = at public expense; **redimo** 3 **redemi** = ransom; **quadriremis quadriremis** 3f = quadrireme (a type of ship); **fluctuo** 1 = float; **salum** 2n = the open sea; **appello** 3 **appuli appulsum** = drive, steer; **istius** = gen of **iste**, "that man there", here referring to Verres, whom Cicero is prosecuting in this case, and who was responsible for the appointment of the incompetent Cleomenes; **invesperascit** 3 impers = evening comes.

Names

Haluntinus adj = (man) of Haluntium, in Sicily; **Locrenses Locrensium** 3 mpl = the Locrians (of Locri, in Sicily); **Apolloniensis Apolloniensis** adj = of Apollonia, in Sicily; **Cleomenes Cleomenis** 3m = Cleomenes; **Helorus** 2m = Helorus, in Sicily; **Heracleo Heracleonis** 3m = Heracleo, a pirate chief.

42. Earlier generals have done no more than temporarily tame the Gauls: Caesar has other ideas.

The war against the Gauls, Senators, which had made little progress previously, has at long last been actively prosecuted by Gaius Caesar.

semper illas nationes nostri imperatores **refutandas** potius bello quam lacessandas putaverunt. ipse ille C. Marius, cuius divina atque **eximia** virtus magnis populi Romani luctibus subvenit, **influentes** in Italiam Gallorum maximas copias **repressit**; non ipse ad eorum urbes sedesque **penetravit**. **modo** ille meorum laborum periculorum consiliorum socius, C.Pomptinus, fortissimus vir, ortum repente bellum **Allobrogum proeliis fregit,** eosque **domuit** qui lacessierant, et ea victoria contentus, re publica metu liberata, quievit. C.Caesaris **longe aliam** video fuisse rationem; non enim sibi solum cum iis quos iam armatos contra populum Romanum videbat bellandum esse **duxit**, sed totam Galliam **in** nostram **dicionem** esse **redigendam**.

Cicero, Concerning the Consular Provinces 32

Words

refuto 1 = drive back; **eximius** adj = outstanding; **influo** 3 = flow (into); **reprimo 3 repressi** = hold back; **penetro** 1 = penetrate; **modo** (here) = recently; **proeliis fregit** = "(he) put an end to by military action"; **domo 3 domui** = overcome; **longe alius** = very different; **duco 3 duxi** (here) = think; **in...dicionem...redigo 3** = bring [someone/something] under [someone's] control.

Names

Allobroges Allobrogum 3mpl = the Allobroges (a Gallic tribe).

43. Another attempt by Verres' henchmen to steal a statue of a river-god from a temple is foiled by the quick action of the temple guards and the local people.

While Verres' men were trying to pull down the statue, all the people of Agrigentum suddenly assembled at the temple. They hurled stones at the robbers, and they - those nocturnal soldiers of that illustrious general of ours - were driven off, taking no more than a couple of small statues.

hanc virtutem **Agrigentinorum** imitati sunt **Assorini** postea, viri fortes et fideles, sed nequaquam ex tam **ampla** civitate. **Chrysas** est amnis qui per **Assorinorum** agros fluit; is apud eos deus **habetur**, et religione maxima colitur. **fanum** eius est in agro, **propter** ipsam viam **qua Assoro itur Hennam**; in eo **Chrysae** simulacrum est, praeclare factum ex marmore. id **iste** poscere **Assorinos** propter singularem eius fani religionem non ausus est; **Tlepolemo** dat et **Hieroni** negotium. illi noctu, facta manu armataque, fores aedis **effringunt**; custodes mature sentiunt; signum, quod erat notum **vicinitati**, **bucina** datur; homines ex agris concurrunt; eicitur fugaturque **Tlepolemus**, neque quicquam ex fano **Chrysae** praeter unum perparvulum **signum** ex aere **desideratum est**.

Cicero, Against Verres II.4.96

Words

amplus adj = large; **habeo** 2 (here) = think, consider; **fanum** 2n = temple; **propter** (+ acc) (here) = alongside; **qua...itur** = "by which one goes..."; **iste** = the defendant in this case, Verres; **effringo** 3 = break down; **vicinitas vicinitatis** 3f = the (people of) the neighbourhood; **bucina** 1f = trumpet; **signum** 2n (here) = statue; **desidero** 1 = lose.

Names

Agrigentini 2mpl = the people of Agrigentum, in Sicily; **Assorini** 2mpl = the people of **Assorum** (2n); **Chrysas Chrysae** m = the river Chrysas, and the god of that river; **Henna** 1f = Henna, a place in Sicily; **Tlepolemus** 2m and **Hiero Hieronis** 3m are two associates of Verres.

44. Cicero warns the people that Antony, like a hunted animal, is at his most dangerous now that he is cornered.

Just as generals before a battle, though they see that their men are already keen to fight, still add further words of encouragement, so shall I, though I know that you are ready and eager, still urge you on to the recovery of your liberty.

non est vobis, **Quirites**, cum eo hoste certamen cum quo **aliqua pacis condicio** esse possit. neque enim ille servitutem vestram, ut antea, sed iam iratus sanguinem concupivit. nullus ei ludus videtur esse iucundior quam cruor, quam caedes, quam ante oculos **trucidatio** civium. **non est res cum** scelerato homine ac nefario, sed cum immani **taetra**que belua. quae, quoniam in **foveam** incidit, **obruatur**. si enim illinc emerserit, **nullius supplicii crudelitas erit recusanda**. sed tenetur, premitur, urgetur nunc iis copiis quas habemus, mox iis quas, paucis diebus, novi consules comparabunt. **incumbite in causam, Quirites**, ut facitis. numquam maior consensus vester in ulla causa fuit, numquam tam vehementer cum senatu **consociati** fuistis. **nec mirum**: agitur enim non **qua condicione** victuri, sed victurine simus an cum suppliciis ignominiaque perituri.

Cicero, Philippic IV.11

Words

aliqua pacis condicio = some kind of peace treaty; **trucidatio trucidationis** 3f = butchery; **non est res cum** = "our battle is not with..."; **taeter** adj = abominable; **fovea** 1f = pit, trap; **obruatur** = "let him be buried"; **nullius...recusanda** = "there is no kind of cruelty to which he will not have recourse"; **incumbite in causam** = rally to the cause; **consociatus** adj = allied; **nec mirum** = and no wonder; **qua condicione** = how.

Names

Quirites Quiritium 3mpl = (Roman) citizens.

45. When people begin to notice that Verres is not executing as many pirates as he captures, he executes some Roman citizens to make up the numbers.

Verres had taken for himself any of the pirates or their slaves who were worth having because of their looks or because they had some particular skill. But eventually people realised that not many of the pirates had been executed, and Verres had to supply the deficiency.

cum magnus numerus deesset, tum iste homo nefarius **substituere** coepit cives Romanos quos in carcerem antea coniecerat; quorum alios **Sertorianos milites** fuisse dicebat; alios, qui a praedonibus erant capti cum **mercaturas** facerent aut aliam ob causam navigarent, **sua voluntate** cum piratis fuisse **arguit**. itaque alii cives Romani, ne cognoscerentur, capitibus **obvolutis** e carcere ad **necem** rapiebantur, alii, **cum** a multis civibus Romanis cognoscerentur, ab omnibus defenderentur, **securi feriebantur**. haec igitur est gesta res, haec victoria praeclara: **myoparone** piratico capto, dux liberatus, **formosi** homines et adulescentes et artifices domum abducti, cives Romani hostilem in modum **cruciati** et necati, omne aurum et argentum ablatum.

Cicero, Against Verres II.5.72

Words

substituo 3 = substitute; **mercatura** 1f = trade, business; **sua voluntate** = of their own volition; **arguo** 3 **argui** = argue, maintain; **obvolutus** adj = covered; **nex necis** 3f = death; **cum** (here) = although; **securi ferio** 4 = execute; **myoparo myoparonis** 3m = ship; **formosus** adj = good-looking; **crucio** 1 = torture.

Names

Sertoriani milites = soldiers of Sertorius (the leader of a rebellion which had recently been suppressed).

46. The poet tells his girlfriend that she is the only one for him.

*No other woman shall seduce me from your bed: this was the promise I
made when we first fell in love, and I keep it still:*

tu mihi sola places, nec iam te praeter in urbe
   formosa est oculis ulla puella meis.
(atque utinam posses **uni mihi** bella videri!
   displiceas aliis! sic ego tutus ero.)
tu mihi curarum requies, tu **nocte vel atra**
   lumen, et in **solis** tu mihi **turba** locis.
nunc **licet** e caelo mittatur amica Tibullo,
   mittetur frustra, **deficiet**que **Venus**.
hoc tibi **sancta** tuae **Iunonis numina** iuro,
   quae sola ante alios est mihi magna deos.
*   "Tibullus" III.19.2.*

Words

uni mihi = to me alone; **displiceas** = may you be displeasing to...;
nocte...atra = "even in the darkest night"; **solus** adj (here) = lonely;
turba 1f (here) = company; **licet** + subj = even if; **deficiet...Venus** =
(lit) Venus will fail me: "I shall not be able to make love";
sancta...numina = "by the holy divinity..."

Names

Iuno Iunonis 3f = the goddess Juno, who represents marriage and
fidelity.

47. An appeal to Phoebus Apollo to come and cure Cerinthus' girlfriend, who is sick. Cerinthus does not know whether to pray or curse, but all will be well.

Come here now, Apollo with your long golden hair; come, and drive away the sickness from this delicate girl.

crede mihi, propera! nec te iam, Phoebe, pigebit
  formosae medicas applicuisse manus.
sancte, veni! tecumque feras quicumque sapores,
  quicumque et cantus corpora fessa levant.
neu iuvenem torque, metuit qui fata puellae,
  votaque pro domina vix numeranda facit.
interdum vovet, interdum, quod langueat illa,
  dicit in aeternos aspera verba deos.
pone metum, Cerinthe: deus non laedit amantes;
  tu modo semper ama: salva puella tibi est.
                    "Tibullus" III.3.10

Words

nec te....pigebit = and you will not regret; **formosa** 1f = a beautiful girl; **medicus** adj = healing; **applico** 1 **applicui** = apply; **tecum...feras** (subj) = "bring with you..."; **quicumque** (adj) = whatever; **sapor saporis** 3m (here) = ointment ; **neu** = et ne; **vix numeranda** = almost innumerable; **langueo** 2 = am ill; **pono** 3 (here) = put aside.

47

48. Ovid advises deserted lovers to make sure they have company to prevent them becoming desperate.

You deserted lovers, beware of solitude! Where are you off to? You'll be safer where there are people. Desolate places are the last thing you want: crowds will do you good.

tristis eris, si solus eris, dominaeque relictae
  ante oculos facies stabit, **ut ipsa**, tuos.
tristior idcirco nox est quam **tempora Phoebi**:
  quae **relevet** luctus turba **sodalis** abest.
nec fuge colloquium, nec sit tibi ianua clausa,
  nec tenebris vultus, **flebilis**, abde tuos.
semper habe **Pyladen** aliquem **qui curet Oresten**:
  hic quoque amicitiae non levis usus erit.
quid nisi **secretae** laeserunt **Phyllida** silvae?
  certa **necis** causa est: **incomitata** fuit.
Phyllidis exemplo **nimium secreta** timete,
  laese vir a domina, laesa puella viro.

Ovid, The Cure for Love 579

Words

ut ipsa = as if she were there in person; **tempora Phoebi** = the daytime; **relevo** 1 = alleviate; **sodalis** adj = of friends; **flebilis** adj = weeping, tearful; **qui curet** = to look after; **secretus** adj = secluded; **nex necis** 3f = death; **incomitatus** adj = unaccompanied; **nimium secreta** = excessively secluded places; **laese** is vocative of the perfect participle of **laedo**: "you (man) who have been hurt..."

Names

Pylades (acc **Pyladen**) and **Orestes** (acc **Oresten**) were proverbially close friends; **Phyllis Phyllidis** 3f (acc **Phyllida**) hanged herself from a tree because she thought her lover Demophoon had abandoned her.

49. Don't leave your lover alone: look what happened when Menelaus left his wife Helen alone with Paris.

Even Penelope was sorely tried by the absence of Ulysses, as was Laodamia by that of Protesilaus. If you must go away, make it short: love fades with absence, and new love can easily take its place.

dum Menelaus abest, **Helene**, ne sola iaceret,
  hospitis est tepido nocte recepta sinu.
quis **stupor** hic, Menelae, fuit? tu solus abibas,
  isdem sub tectis hospes et uxor erant!
nil **Helene** peccat, nihil **hic** committit **adulter**:
  quod tu, **quod faceret quilibet**, ille facit.
cogis **adulterium** dando tempusque locumque;
  quid nisi consilio est usa puella tuo?
quid faciat? vir abest, et adest non rusticus hospes,
  et timet in vacuo sola **cubare** toro.
viderit Atrides: **Helenen** ego crimine **solvo**:
  usa est **humani commoditate viri**!

                Ovid, The Art of Love II.359

Words

stupor stuporis 3m = madness, stupidity; **hic...adulter** = this so-called adulterer; **quod...quilibet** = what anyone would do; **adulterium** 2n = adultery; **cubo** 1 = sleep; **viderit Atrides** = "Menelaus should have had more sense"; **solvo** 3 (here) = absolve; **humanus** adj (here) = indulgent; **commoditas commoditatis** 3f = kindness, laxity; **vir** (here) = husband.

Names

Helene (acc **Helenen**) f = Helen; **Atrides Atridis** 3m = son of Atreus: Menelaus.

50. A boy who wants a girlfriend must know where to look, but he need not go far.

While you have nothing to tie you down, look around for a girl you can fall in love with:

haec tibi non tenues veniet **delapsa** per auras:
  quaerenda est oculis apta puella tuis.
scit bene **venator, cervis** ubi **retia tendat**;
  scit bene qua **frendens** valle moretur aper:
tu quoque, **materiam** longo qui quaeris amori,
  ante frequens quo sit disce puella loco.
non ego **quaerentem** vento dare vela iubebo,
  nec tibi ut invenias longa **terenda** via est.
Andromedan Perseus nigris **portarit** ab **Indis**;
  raptaque sit Phrygio Graia puella viro:
tot tibi tamque dabit formosas Roma puellas
  "haec habet" ut dicas, "quidquid in orbe fuit."
                    Ovid, the Art of Love I.43

Words

delapsa = "gliding down"; **venator venatoris** 3m = hunter; **cervus** 2m stag; **retia** 3npl = nets; **tendo** 3 (here) = spread; **frendeo** 2 = gnash one's teeth; **materia** 1f = object; **ante...loco** = "first find out where there are a lot of girls"; **quaerentem** = "you who are searching"; **tero** 3 = tread, travel; **portarit** and **rapta sit**: these subjunctives may be translated "although ..."

Names

Andromeda f (acc **Andromedan**) = Andromeda; **Perseus** m = Perseus; **Indi** 2mpl = the Indians; **Phrygius vir** = Paris; **Graia puella** = Helen.

51. Some of Caesar's men almost get caught in a Gallic town while negotiating its surrender.

Caesar sent in the legions that he had ordered to stand by, and occupied the town. The enemy were very nearly all captured, as the narrowness of the bridge and the roads had prevented most of them from escaping.

oppidum diripit atque incendit, praedam militibus donat, exercitum **Ligerim** traducit atque in **Biturigum** fines pervenit. **Vercingetorix**, ubi de Caesaris adventu cognovit, oppugnatione destitit atque obviam Caesari proficiscitur. ille oppidum **Biturigum** positum in via oppugnare instituerat. quo ex oppido cum legati ad eum venissent oratum ut sibi ignosceret, arma conferri, equos produci, obsides dari iubet. parte iam obsidum tradita, centurionibus et paucis militibus intromissis qui arma **iumenta**que **conquirerent**, equitatus hostium procul visus est, qui agmen **Vercingetorigis** antecesserat. quem simul atque **oppidani** conspexerunt atque in spem auxilii venerunt, clamore sublato, arma capere, portas claudere, murum complere coeperunt. centuriones in oppido, cum **ex significatione Gallorum novi aliquid** ab eis **iniri consilii** intellexissent, gladiis destrictis, portas occupaverunt suosque omnes incolumes receperunt.

Caesar, Gallic War VII.11

Words

iumentum 2n = pack-animal, mule; **conquiro** 3 = get; **oppidani** 2mpl = townspeople; **ex...Gallorum** = "from what the Gauls were doing"; **novi aliquid consilii** = some new plan; **ineo inire** (here) = adopt.

Names

Liger Ligeris (acc **Ligerim**) 3m = the river Loire; **Bituriges Biturigum** 3m = the Bituriges; **Vercingetorix Vercingetorigis** 3m = Vercingetorix, a Gallic chieftain.

**52. After a fierce skirmish, Caesar discovers why his German
enemy Ariovistus would not risk a pitched battle.**

*Ariovistus sent out about 16,000 infantry and all his cavalry to prevent
our men fortifying a camp. But Caesar stood by his decision, and
ordered two lines of men to repel the enemy and a third to complete the
fortifications.*

munitis castris, duas ibi legiones reliquit et partem **auxiliorum**;
quattuor reliquas in castra maiora reduxit. proximo die Caesar e castris
utrisque copias suas duxit paulumque a maioribus castris progressus
aciem instruxit; hostibus pugnandi potestatem fecit. ubi ne tum quidem
eos **prodire** intellexit, circiter meridiem exercitum in castra reduxit.
tum demum Ariovistus partem suarum copiarum quae castra minora
oppugnaret misit. acriter utrimque usque ad vesperum pugnatum est.
solis occasu suas copias Ariovistus, multis et inlatis et acceptis
vulneribus, in castra reduxit. cum ex captivis quaereret Caesar quam ob
rem Ariovistus proelio non **decertaret**, hanc reperiebat causam: quod
apud Germanos ea consuetudo esset ut matres familiae eorum sortibus
et **vaticinationibus** declararent utrum proelium committi **ex usu** esset
necne; eas ita dicere: non esse fas Germanos superare, si ante novam
lunam proelio contendissent.

Caesar, Gallic War I.49

Words
auxilia 2npl = auxiliaries; **prodeo prodire** = come out; **decerto** 1 =
fight; **vaticinatio vaticinationis** 3f = prophecy; **ex usu** = of use.

53. Orgetorix persuades two other ambitious young princes to plot with him to take over the whole of Gaul.

When the Helvetii had made a decision to migrate, they decided to take two years to make their preparations, and set out in the third.

ad eas res conficiendas Orgetorix deligitur. is sibi legationem ad civitates suscepit. in eo itinere, persuadet **Castico, Sequano,** cuius pater regnum in **Sequanis** multos annos obtinuerat et a senatu "populi Romani amicus" appellatus erat, ut regnum in civitate sua occuparet quod pater ante habuerat; itemque **Dumnorigi Aeduo,** fratri **Diviciaci,** qui eo tempore principatum in civitate obtinebat ac maxime plebi **acceptus** erat, ut idem conaretur persuadet, eique filiam suam in matrimonium dat. **perfacile factu esse illis probat** conata perficere, propterea quod ipse suae civitatis imperium obtenturus esset: non esse dubium quin totius Galliae **plurimum** Helvetii **possent;** se suis copiis suoque exercitu illis regna **conciliaturum** confirmat. hac oratione adducti, inter se fidem et **iusiurandum** dant et, regno occupato per tres potentissimos ac firmissimos populos, totius Galliae sese potiri posse sperant.

Caesar, Gallic War I.3

Words
acceptus adj = popular; **perfacile...probat** = "he convinced them that it would be easy..."; **plurimum posse** = to be most powerful; **concilio** 1 = secure; **iusiurandum iurisiurandi** n = oath.

Names
Casticus 2m = Casticus, a Sequanian (**Sequanus** adj); **Dumnorix Dumnorigis** 3m = Dumnorix, an Aeduan (**Aeduus** adj); **Diviciacus** 2m = Diviciacus, an Aeduan.

53

54. Caesar makes a successful attack on some of the Helvetii, and receives a delegation from them.

There is a river called the Saone which flows into the Rhone between the territory of the Aedui and the Sequani. The Helvetii were crossing it on rafts and small boats tied together.

ubi per exploratores Caesar certior factus est tres iam partes copiarum Helvetiorum id flumen traduxisse, quartam fere partem citra flumen **Ararim** reliquam esse, de tertia vigilia cum legionibus tribus e castris profectus, ad eam partem pervenit quae nondum flumen transierat. eos impeditos et **inopinantes** aggressus, magnam partem eorum concidit: reliqui sese fugae mandarunt atque in proximas silvas abdiderunt. hoc proelio facto, reliquas copias Helvetiorum ut consequi posset, pontem in **Arare** faciendum curat atque ita exercitum traducit. Helvetii, **repentino** eius adventu commoti, legatos ad eum mittunt. cuius legationis **Divico** princeps fuit, qui **bello Cassiano** dux Helvetiorum fuerat. **is ita cum Caesare egit**: si pacem populus Romanus cum Helvetiis faceret, in eam partem ituros atque ibi futuros Helvetios ubi eos Caesar constituisset atque esse voluisset; sin bello persequi perseveraret, **reminisceretur** et veteris **incommodi** populi Romani et pristinae virtutis Helvetiorum.

Caesar, Gallic War I.12

Words

inopinans inopinantis adj = not expecting; **repentinus** adj = sudden; **bello Cassiano** = in the war with Cassius; **is....egit** = "he spoke to Caesar as follows"; **reminiscor** 3dep (+ gen) = remember; **incommodum** 2n = defeat.

Names

Arar Araris 3m = the river Saone; **Divico Diviconis** 3m = Divico.

55. When Pompey refuses him help, Domitius plans a cowardly escape from a siege, but his unusual behaviour brings about the discovery of his plan and causes a mutiny amongst his soldiers.

On the following days, Caesar set about surrounding the town of Corfinium with ramparts and siege-towers. When this work was largely complete, the messengers that Domitius had sent to Pompey asking for help came back with a letter from him.

litteris perlectis, Domitius, **dissimulans**, in concilio pronuntiat Pompeium celeriter subsidio venturum, hortaturque eos ne animo deficiant. ipse **arcano** cum paucis familiaribus suis colloquitur consiliumque fugae capere constituit. cum vultus Domiti cum oratione non consentiret, multumque cum suis **consiliandi** causa secreto praeter consuetudinem colloqueretur, res diutius tegi **dissimulari**que non potuit. Pompeius enim rescripserat sese rem in summum periculum deducturum non esse, neque suo consilio aut voluntate Domitium se in oppidum Corfinium contulisse. **divulgato** Domiti consilio, milites qui erant Corfini primo vesperi secessionem faciunt atque ita inter se colloquuntur: obsideri se a Caesare; **opera** munitionesque prope esse perfectas; ducem suum Domitium, cuius spe atque fiducia permanserint, proiectis omnibus fugae consilium capere; debere se suae salutis rationem habere.

Caesar, Civil War I.19

Words

dissimulo 1 = dissemble, lie, cover up; **arcano** adv = secretly; **consilior** 1dep = confer; **divulgo** 1 = spread about, publicise; **opera** 3npl = defences.

56. The intervention of Publius Crassus changes the course of a battle against the Germans, and results in a personal tragedy for their chieftain Ariovistus.

But the Germans quickly formed up and resisted our onslaught. Quite a number of our men threw themselves on the shield-wall in front of them, tore the shields from the Gauls' hands, and wounded them from above.

cum hostium acies a sinistro cornu pulsa atque in fugam conversa esset, a dextro cornu vehementer multitudine suorum nostram aciem premebant. id cum animadvertisset P.Crassus adulescens, qui equitatui praeerat, quod **expeditior** erat quam ei qui inter aciem versabantur, tertiam aciem **laborantibus** nostris subsidio misit. ita proelium restitutum est, atque omnes hostes terga verterunt, neque prius fugere destiterunt quam ad flumen **Rhenum**, milia passuum ex eo loco circiter quinque, pervenerunt. ibi perpauci aut viribus confisi tranare contenderunt aut **lintribus** inventis sibi salutem reppererunt. in his fuit Ariovistus, qui naviculam **deligatam** ad ripam nactus ea profugit: reliquos omnes equitatu consecuti nostri interfecerunt. duae fuerunt Ariovisti uxores, una **Sueba** natione, quam domo secum duxerat, altera **Norica**, regis **Voccionis** soror, quam in Gallia **duxerat**, a fratre missam: utraeque in ea fuga perierunt; duae filiae; harum altera occisa, altera capta est.

Caesar, Gallic War I.52

Words
expeditus adj = lightly armed; **laboro** 1 (here) = struggle, be in difficulties; **linter lintris** 3f = boat; **deligo** 1 = tie up; **duco** (here) = marry.

Names
Rhenus 2m = the river Rhine; **Suebus** adj = Suebian; **Noricus** adj = Norican; **Voccio Voccionis** 3m = Voccio.

57. Labienus, formerly one of Caesar's officers, reinforces the optimism of Pompey and his men, who are about to fight against Caesar.

Pompey encouraged his men not to let themselves down now that they had the opportunity of fighting that they had been waiting for. Then Labienus addressed them, speaking disparagingly about Caesar's army and praising Pompey's strategy:

"noli" inquit, "existimare, Pompei, hunc esse exercitum qui Galliam Germaniamque devicerit. omnibus **interfui** proeliis, neque temere rem incognitam pronuntio. perexigua pars illius exercitus superest; magna pars deperiit, quod accidere tot proeliis fuit necesse; multi domum discesserunt; multi sunt relicti in continenti. an non audistis ex eis qui per causam valetudinis remanserunt cohortes esse **Brundisi** factas? has copias quas videtis ex **dilectibus** horum annorum in **citeriore Gallia** sunt refectae, et plerique sunt ex **coloniis Transpadanis**." haec cum dixisset, iuravit se nisi victorem in castra non reversurum, reliquosque ut idem facerent cohortatus est. hoc laudans, Pompeius idem iuravit; nec vero ex reliquis fuit quisquam qui iurare dubitaret. haec cum facta sunt in consilio, magna spe et laetitia omnium discessum est, ac iam animo victoriam **praecipiebant**, quod de re tanta et a tam perito imperatore nihil frustra confirmari videbatur.

Caesar, Civil War III.87

Words

intersum interesse interfui (+dat) = take part in; **dilectus** 4m = levy (a conscription of troops); **praecipio** 3 (here) = anticipate.

Names

Brundisium 2n (locative **Brundisi**) = Brundisium (Brindisi); **Gallia citerior** = the nearer part of Gaul; **coloniae Transpadanae** 1fpl = the colonies on the far side of the river Po.

58. In his first encounter with the Britons, Caesar has some problems with their guerilla tactics, but manages to drive them from their stronghold.

He reached Britain about midday, and no enemy was in sight: he found out later that a force had assembled, but had retreated and concealed itself in the woods, terrified by the number of Caesar's ships.

Caesar, exposito exercitu et loco castris idoneo capto, ubi ex captivis cognovit quo in loco hostium copiae consedissent, cohortibus decem ad mare relictis et equitibus trecentis qui praesidio navibus essent, de tertia vigilia ad hostes contendit, et praesidio navibus Q.Atrium praefecit. ipse, noctu progressus milia passuum circiter XII, hostium copias conspicatus est. illi, equitatu atque **essedis** ad flumen progressi, ex loco superiore proelium committere coeperunt. repulsi ab equitatu, se in silvas abdiderunt, locum nacti egregie et natura et opere munitum; nam, crebris arboribus succisis, omnes introitus erant **praeclusi**. ipsi ex silvis **rari** propugnabant, nostrosque intra munitiones ingredi prohibebant. at milites legionis septimae, **testudine** facta et aggere ad munitiones **adiecto**, locum ceperunt eosque ex silvis expulerunt, paucis vulneribus acceptis. sed eos fugientes longius Caesar prosequi vetuit, et quod loci naturam ignorabat et quod, magna parte diei consumpta, munitioni castrorum tempus relinqui volebat.

Caesar, Gallic War V.9

Words

essedum 2n = chariot; **praecludo** 3 **praeclusi praeclusum** = block; **rari** = scattered, in small groups; **testudo testudinis** 3f = a "tortoise", the military formation in which soldiers advanced holding their shields over their heads; **adicio** 3 **adieci adiectum** = put up.

59. Pompey reaches Egypt after defeat by Caesar, and is treacherously murdered by the followers of King Ptolemy, with the assistance of some Romans in Ptolemy's service.

As it happened, the young King Ptolemy was at Pelusium. He was waging war on his sister Cleopatra, whom he had managed to drive out a few months previously.

ad eum Pompeius misit, ut **pro** amicitia patris **Alexandria** reciperetur atque illius opibus tegeretur. sed qui ab eo missi erant cum militibus regis colloqui coeperunt eosque hortari ut suum **officium** Pompeio **praestarent**, neve eius fortunam despicerent. (in hoc erant numero complures Pompei milites, quos, ex eius exercitu acceptos in Syria, **Gabinius Alexandriam** traduxerat.) his tunc cognitis rebus, amici regis, qui propter aetatem eius **in procuratione** erant regni, sive timore adducti ne Pompeius **Alexandriam Aegyptum**que occuparet, sive despecta eius fortuna, eis qui erant ab eo missi palam **liberaliter** responderunt, eumque ad regem venire iusserunt: ipsi, clam consilio inito, **Achillam**, praefectum regium, singulari hominem audacia, et L.Septimium, tribunum militum, ad interficiendum Pompeium miserunt. ab his **liberaliter** appellatus, naviculam conscendit cum paucis suis; ibi ab **Achilla** et Septimio interficitur.

Caesar, Civil War III.103

Words

pro (+abl) (here) = because of; **officium praesto** 1 = do one's duty; **in procuratione** = in charge; **liberaliter** adv = in a friendly way.

Names

Alexandria 1f = Alexandria, in Egypt (**Aegyptus** 2f); **Gabinius** 2m = Gabinius, a Roman officer; **Achillas** 1m (abl **Achilla**) = Achillas, an Egyptian general.

60. Caesar's strategy cuts off Pompey from his base at Dyrrachium.

When he knew that Caesar and Antony had joined forces, Pompey left that place and went to Asparagium with all his forces, so as not to be blocked in by their two armies.

Caesar, postquam Pompeium ad Asparagium esse cognovit, **eodem** cum exercitu profectus, tertio die ad Pompeium pervenit iuxtaque eum castra posuit et postridie, eductis omnibus copiis, acie instructa, **decernendi** potestatem Pompeio fecit. ubi illum suis locis se tenere **animum advertit**, reducto in castra exercitu, aliud sibi consilium capiendum existimavit. itaque postero die, omnibus copiis, difficili angustoque itinere, Dyrrachium profectus est, sperans Pompeium aut Dyrrachium compelli aut ab eo **intercludi** posse, quod omnem commeatum totiusque belli apparatum eo contulisset; ut accidit. Pompeius enim, primo ignorans eius consilium, **angustiis** rei frumentariae compulsum discessisse existimabat; postea per exploratores certior factus, postero die castra movit, breviore itinere se occurrere ei posse sperans. quod fore suspicatus Caesar, militesque adhortatus ut **aequo animo** laborem ferrent, parva parte noctis itinere **intermisso**, mane Dyrrachium venit, cum primum agmen Pompei procul cerneretur, atque ibi castra posuit.

Caesar, Civil War III.41

Words

eodem = to the same place; **decerno** 3 = fight it out; **animum advertit** = **animadvertit**; **intercludo** 3 = cut off; **angustiae** 1fpl = shortage; **aequo animo** = patiently; **intermitto** 3 **intermisi intermissum** = interrupt.

61. Hypermnestra and her sisters were told by their father Danaus to kill their newly wedded husbands. But she fell in love with hers, Lynceus, and helped him to escape. She writes to him from prison.

While I was saying this, I began to weep, and my tears fell on your body. You sleepily moved your arms towards me and tried to embrace me, and nearly wounded yourself on my sword.

iamque patrem **famulos**que patris lucemque timebam;
  expulerunt somnos haec mea dicta tuos:
"surge age, **Belide**, de tot modo fratribus unus!
  nox tibi, ni properas, ista **perennis** erit!"
territus exsurgis; fugit omnis inertia somni;
  adspicis in timida fortia tela manu.
quaerenti causam, "dum nox sinit, effuge!" dixi.
  dum nox atra sinit, tu fugis, ipsa moror.
mane erat et Danaus **generos** ex caede iacentes
  dinumerat: summae criminis unus abes.
abstrahor a patriis pedibus, raptamque capillis
  (haec meruit pietas praemia!) carcer habet.

                Ovid, Heroides XIV.71

Words
famulus 2m = servant; **perennis** adj = everlasting; **gener generi** 2m = son-in-law.
Names
Belides Belidis 3m = son of Belus (Lynceus).

62. Two fishes save Dione (Venus) and her son Cupid when they are pursued by a giant. Their reward is to become the constellation Pisces; and the inhabitants of the region where this happened do not eat this kind of fish.

The story is that you and your brother fish carried two gods on your backs:

terribilem quondam fugiens **Typhona** Dione
  (**tunc cum pro caelo Iuppiter arma tulit**),
venit ad **Euphratem, comitata** Cupidine parvo,
  inque **Palaestinae** margine sedit aquae.
populus et **cannae** riparum summa tenebant,
  spemque dabant **salices** hos quoque posse tegi.
dum latet, **insonuit** vento nemus; illa timore
  pallet et hostiles credit adesse manus,
utque sinu tenuit natum, "succurrite, nymphae,
  et dis auxilium ferte duobus!" ait.
nec mora, prosiluit; pisces subiere **gemelli**:
  pro quo nunc dignum sidera munus habent.
inde nefas **ducunt** genus hoc imponere mensis
  nec violant timidi piscibus ora **Syri**.

Ovid, Fasti II.261

Words

tunc...tulit: the reference is to the war of Jupiter against the Giants; **comitatus** adj = accompanied; **populus** 2f = poplar; **canna** 1f = reed; **salix salicis** 3f = willow; **insono 1 insonui** = make a noise; **gemelli pl** adj = twin; **duco** 3 (here) = consider.

Names

Typhon (acc **Typhona**) = Typhon, a giant; **Euphrates Euphratis** 3m = the river Euphrates; **Palaestinus** adj = of Palestine; **Syri** 2mpl = the Syrians.

63. **Carmentis consoles her exiled son by telling him that other great men have suffered a similar fate. Together they journey to Italy.**

When Evander was forced to leave his homeland, he feared the worst. But as he wept, his mother said, "Dry your tears, I pray: you must bear your fortune like a man.

sic erat in fatis, nec te tua culpa fugavit,
  sed deus; offenso pulsus es urbe deo.
nec tamen ut primus maere mala talia passus:
  obruit ingentes ista **procella** viros.
passus idem **Tydeus**, et idem **Pagasaeus Iason**,
  et quos praeterea longa referre mora est.
nec fera tempestas toto tamen **horret** in anno,
  et tibi, crede mihi, tempora veris erunt."
vocibus Evander **firmata** mente parentis
  nave **secat** fluctus, **Hesperiam**que tenet.
iamque ratem, doctae **monitu** Carmentis, in amnem
  egerat, et **Tuscis obvius** ibat aquis.
puppibus egressus, **Latia** stetit exsul in herba;
  felix, exsilium cui locus ille fuit!
                    Ovid, Fasti I.481

Words

obruo 3 **obrui** = overwhelm; **procella** 1f = storm; **horreo** 2 (here) = seethe, rage; **firmo** 1 = strengthen, confirm; **seco** 1 = cut through; **monitus** 4m = advice; **obvius** = **obviam**.

Names

Tydeus and **Iason** (Jason) are Greek heroes; **Pagasaeus** adj = from Pagasa, in Greece; **Hesperia** 1f = Italy; **Tuscus** adj = Tuscan; **Latius** adj = Latin, of Latium.

63

64. In response to his father's curse, a bull out of the sea terrifies Hippolytus' horses and brings about his death. Aesculapius resurrects him, for which he is punished by Jupiter, who later relents and makes Aesculapius a god.

Everyone knows how Phaedra fell in love with her stepson Hippolytus, and how, when he refused her, she told Theseus that he had tried to rape her; and how Theseus believed her accusations, and cursed his son. The doomed young man set off for Troezen in his chariot, when suddenly a bull appeared out of the sea:

solliciti terrentur equi, frustraque retenti,
   per scopulos dominum duraque saxa trahunt.
exciderat curru **loris**que morantibus artus
   Hippolytus **lacero** corpore raptus erat,
reddideratque animam, multum **indignante Diana**.
   "nulla" **Coronides** "causa doloris," ait;
"namque pio iuveni vitam sine vulnere reddam,
   et cedent arti tristia fata meae."
pectora ter tetigit, ter verba **salubria** dixit:
   depositum terra sustulit ille caput.
Iuppiter, exemplum veritus, **direxit** in ipsum
   fulmina, qui nimiae noverat artis opem.
Phoebe, querebaris: deus est, **placare** parenti:
   propter te, fieri quod vetat, ipse facit.
                         Ovid, Fasti VI.739

Words
sollicitus adj = alarmed; **lora** 2npl = reins; **lacer lacera lacerum** adj = torn; **indignor** 1dep = resent; **salubris** adj = health-giving; **dirigo** 3 **direxi** = direct; **placor** 1pass (+dat) = be reconciled to.
Names
Diana 1f = the goddess Diana, of whom Hippolytus had been a devotee; **Coronides** 3m = son of Coronis (Aesculapius, son of Coronis and **Phoebus** 2m).

65. The shipwrecked friends Orestes and Pylades are about to be sacrificed by a Scythian priestess. She offers to save one of them to take a message to her brother, who turns out to be Orestes himself.

While the priestess prepared them for sacrifice, she said, "Forgive me: I am not myself cruel; it is the custom of the land. But where are you from? And where were you journeying to ?"

dixit, et audito patriae pia nomine virgo
  consortes urbis **comperit** esse suae.
"**alteruter** nostris", inquit, "cadat hostia sacris,
  ad patrias sedes nuntius alter eat."
ire iubet Pylades carum, periturus, **Oresten**;
  hic negat, **inque vices** pugnat uterque mori.
dum peragunt pulchri iuvenes certamen amoris,
  ad fratrem **scriptas exarat** illa **notas**.
ad fratrem mandata dabat: cuique illa dabantur
  (humanos casus adspice!) frater erat.
nec mora, de templo rapiunt **simulacra Dianae**,
  clamque per immensas puppe feruntur aquas.
mirus amor iuvenum; quamvis abiere tot anni,
  in Scythia magnum nunc quoque nomen habent.
        Ovid, Letters from Pontus III.2.81

Words
consors consortis 3m = fellow-countryman;**comperio 3 comperi** = find out; **alteruter** = one or the other; **in...vices** = in turn, against each other; **exaro 1** (here) = write; **scriptae...notae** 1fpl = a letter.
Names
Orestes (acc **Oresten**) = Orestes, who has been commanded to take the **simulacra Dianae** back to Greece.

65

66. Icarus flies too near the sun and falls into the Icarian Sea, which is named after him.

Daedalus flapped his own wings and looked back to see how his son was flying. Icarus was beginning to enjoy the new sensation, and soon he stopped being afraid and began to fly more confidently.

iam **Samos** a laeva (fuerant **Naxos**que relictae,
  et **Paros** et **Clario Delos** amata **deo**),
cum puer, incautis nimium **temerarius** annis,
  altius egit iter, deseruitque patrem.
vincla **labant** et **cera, deo propiore,** liquescit,
  nec tenues ventos bracchia mota tenent.
territus, a summo despexit in aequora caelo;
  nox oculis pavido venit **oborta** metu.
tabuerant cerae: nudus **quatit** ille lacertos
  et trepidat, nec quo sustineatur habet.
decidit, atque cadens, "pater, o pater! auferor!" inquit;
  clauserunt virides ora loquentis aquae.
at pater infelix, nec iam pater, "Icare!" clamat,
  "Icare!" clamat, "ubi es, quoque sub axe volas?
Icare!" clamabat; pennas aspexit in undis.
  ossa tegit tellus: aequora nomen habent.
Ovid, The Art of Love II.79

Words

temerarius adj = rash; **labo** 1 = come apart; **cera** 1f = wax (which Daedalus used to construct their wings); **deus** (here) = the sun; **propior** comp adj = too near; **nox** (here) = darkness, panic; **oborior** 4dep **obortus sum** = arise; **tabesco** 3 **tabui** = melt; **quatio** 3 = flap.

Names

Samos, Naxos, Paros, and **Delos** (all f) are islands; Delos was sacred to Apollo (**Clarius deus** 2m).

67. Laodamia writes to Protesilaus to tell him how she watched him and his ship sailing away.

There is a rumour that you are delayed at Aulis by adverse winds: where were these adverse winds when you hurried away from me?

tum freta debuerant vestris **obsistere** remis:
　illud erat saevis utile tempus aquis.
oscula plura viro **mandata**que plura dedissem;
　et sunt quae volui dicere multa tibi.
ventus erat nautis aptus, non aptus amanti:
　solvor ab amplexu, Protesilae, tuo.
incubuit Boreas abreptaque vela **tetendit**,
　iamque meus longe Protesilaus erat.
dum potui spectare virum, spectare iuvabat,
　sumque tuos oculos **usque** secuta meis;
ut te non poteram, poteram tua vela videre:
　vela diu vultus detinuere meos;
at postquam nec te nec vela fugacia vidi,
　et quod spectarem nil nisi pontus erat,
lux quoque tecum abiit, tenebrisque **exsanguis** obortis
　succiduo dicor **procubuisse** genu.

Ovid, Heroides XIII.5

Words

obsisto 3 (+dat) = resist, obstruct; **mandata** 2npl = instructions; **incumbo** 3 **incubui** = grow strong; **tendo** 3 **tetendi** (here) = spread; **usque** = "as far as I could"; **exsanguis** adj = unconscious; **succiduus** adj = giving way; **procumbo** 3 **procubui** = collapse.

Names

Boreas 1m = the North Wind.

68. Some slaves are ordered to drown the new-born Romulus and Remus, but they cannot bring themselves to carry out their orders fully, and the babies survive.

The Vestal Virgin Silvia bore two sons to the god Mars. Her uncle the King ordered them to be taken away and drowned in the river.

iussa recusantes peragunt lacrimosa ministri
  (flent tamen) et geminos in loca iussa ferunt.
huc ubi venerunt (neque enim procedere possunt
  longius), ex illis unus an alter ait:
"at quam sunt similes! at quam formosus uterque!
  plus tamen ex illis iste vigoris habet.
si genus **arguitur** vultu, nisi fallit imago,
  nescioquem in vobis suspicor esse deum -
at si quis vestrae deus esset originis auctor,
  in tam **praecipiti** tempore ferret opem.
nata simul, moritura simul, simul ite sub undas
  corpora!" **desierat, deposuit**que **sinu.**
sustinet impositos summa cavus alveus unda:
  heu, quantum fati parva **tabella** tulit!
alveus in **limo** silvis appulsus opacis
  paulatim, fluvio deficiente, sedet.

Ovid, Fasti II.387

Words

iussa 2npl = orders; **recusantes** = reluctantly; **arguo** 3 = show;
praeceps praecipitis adj (here) = dangerous; **desierat** = **desiverat**;
deposuit...sinu = "[he] put them down"; **tabella** 1f = piece of wood (i.e.
the cradle in which Romulus and Remus are); **limus** 2m = mud.

69. Dido writes to Aeneas to say that, if he must leave her, he has at least provided her with the means to die.

I do not hope for marriage now, but give me a little more time until the seas grow calmer and until my love grows less and I can learn to bear the pain of separation.

si minus, est animus nobis effundere vitam;
  in me crudelis non potes esse diu.
adspicias utinam quae sit scribentis imago:
  scribimus, et gremio Troicus ensis adest,
perque genas lacrimae strictum labuntur in ensem
  qui iam pro lacrimis sanguine tinctus erit.
quam bene conveniunt fato tua munera nostro!
  instruis impensa nostra sepulcra brevi.
nec mea nunc primum feriuntur pectora telo;
  ille locus saevi vulnus amoris habet.
Anna soror, soror Anna, meae male conscia culpae,
  iam dabis in cineres ultima dona meos,
nec, consumpta rogis, inscribar "Elissa Sychaei";
  hoc tantum in tumuli marmore carmen erit:
"praebuit Aeneas et causam mortis et ensem;
  ipsa sua Dido concidit usa manu."

                 Ovid, Heroides VII.181

Words
si minus = if not; quae...imago = "what I look like as I write"; gremium 2n = lap; tingo 3 tinxi tinctum = stain; convenio 4 (here) = suit, be appropriate; impensa 1f = expenditure; sepulcra 2npl (here) = funeral, death; conscius adj = sharing knowledge.

Names
Troicus adj = Trojan; Elissa (1f) is another name for Dido; Sychaeus 2m = Sychaeus, Dido's former husband.

70. According to a promise made by Jupiter to King Numa, a shield falls from the sky as a guarantee of Rome's future empire.

The people waited for the following day for confirmation of what the King had said. The ground was still damp from the morning frost when they assembled outside the palace waiting for the King to come out.

prodit, et in **solio** medius consedit **acerno**:
  innumeri circa stantque **silent**que viri.
ortus erat summo **tantummodo margine Phoebus**:
  sollicitae mentes speque metuque pavent.
constitit atque, caput **niveo velatus amictu**,
  iam bene dis notas sustulit ille manus,
atque ita "tempus adest promissi muneris," inquit;
  "pollicitam dictis, Iuppiter, adde fidem".
dum loquitur, totum iam sol emoverat orbem,
  et gravis aetherio venit ab axe **fragor**.
ter **tonuit** sine nube deus, tria **fulgura** misit.
  (credite dicenti! mira, sed acta, loquor.)
a media caelum regione **dehiscere** coepit;
  summisere oculos cum duce turba suo.
ecce! levi scutum **versatum** leniter aura
  decidit: a populo clamor ad astra venit.
                    Ovid, Fasti III.361

Words

prodeo prodire = come out; **solium** 2n = throne; **acernus** adj = of maple; **sileo** 2 = be silent; **tantummodo** adv = just; **margo marginis** 3m (here) = horizon; **niveus** adj = white; **velo** 1 = veil; **amictus** 4m = garment; **fragor fragoris** 3m = crash; **tono** 1 **tonui** = thunder; **fulgur fulguris** 3n = flash of lightning; **dehisco** 3 = split open; **versatus** (here) = turning over, rotating.

Names

Phoebus 2m (here) = the sun.

71. The Romans repel a Volscian invasion.

The plebeians had been at odds with the senators because many had been sold into slavery through debts incurred while fighting for their country. When a Volscian invasion threatened, the consul published an edict outlawing this practice. Released debtors rushed to enlist, and no troops were more enthusiastic in the war.

consul copias contra hostem educit; parvo **dirimente** intervallo castra ponit. proxima inde nocte Volsci, discordia Romana freti, **si** qua nocturna **transitio** proditiove fieri posset, temptant castra. sensere vigiles; excitatus exercitus; signo dato, concursum est ad arma; ita frustra id inceptum Volscis fuit. reliquum noctis utrimque quieti datum. postero die prima luce Volsci, fossis repletis, vallum invadunt. iamque ab omni parte munimenta vellebantur, cum consul, quamquam cuncti (et **nexi** ante omnes) ut signum daret clamabant, experiendi animos militum causa parumper moratus, postquam satis apparebat ingens ardor, dato tandem ad erumpendum signo, militem avidum certaminis emittit. primo statim incursu pulsi hostes; fugientibus, quoad insequi pedes potuit, terga caesa; eques usque ad castra pavidos egit. mox, ipsa castra, legionibus circumdatis, cum Volscos inde etiam pavor expulisset, capta direptaque.

Livy II.24

Words

dirimo 3 = intervene, be between; **si** (here) = in case; **transitio transitionis** 3f = desertion; **nexi** 2mpl = the debtors.

72. A fatal single combat between Arruns Tarquinius, the son of the exiled King of Rome, and the consul Brutus, who had been responsible for his exile.

So two armies from two states accompanied King Tarquin on his expedition against Rome, in an attempt to regain his kingdom for him.

postquam in agrum Romanum ventum est, obviam hosti consules eunt. Valerius **quadrato agmine** peditem ducit: Brutus ad explorandum cum equitatu antecessit. eodem modo primus eques hostium agminis fuit; praeerat Arruns Tarquinius filius regis; rex ipse cum legionibus sequebatur. Arruns, ubi **ex lictoribus** procul consulem esse, deinde iam propius ac certius facie quoque Brutum cognovit, inflammatus ira, "ille est vir," inquit, "qui nos **extorres** expulit patria! ipse (en!) ille nostris decoratus **insignibus** magnifice incedit. di regum ultores adeste!" concitat **calcaribus** equum atque in ipsum infestus consulem derigit. sensit in se iri Brutus; **decorum erat tum** ipsis **capessere** pugnam ducibus; avide itaque se certamini offert; adeoque infestis animis concurrerunt, neuter dum hostem vulneraret sui protegendi corpus memor, ut **contrario ictu** per **parmam** uterque transfixus, moribundi ex equis lapsi sint.

Livy II.6

Words

quadrato agmine = in square formation; **ex lictoribus** = "because of his lictors" (the consul's bodyguard); **extorris extorris** 3m = exile; **insignia** 3npl = insignia, honours; **calcar calcaris** 3n = spur; **decorum...tum** = "it was considered honourable in those days"; **capesso** 3 = **capio** (here = take part in); **contrario ictu** = by each other's blows; **parma** 1f = shield.

73. King Syphax of Numidia is encouraged by the Romans to maintain his hostility to Carthage. In return he asks that a Roman officer be left with him as a military adviser.

In the same year, Publius and Gnaeus Scipio, since things had gone well for them in Spain and they had regained their allies and made new ones, turned their attention to Africa.

Syphax erat rex **Numidarum**, subito Carthaginiensibus hostis factus; ad eum centuriones **miserunt** qui cum eo amicitiam societatemque facerent, et pollicerentur, si perseveraret urgere bello Carthaginienses, gratam eam rem fore senatui populoque Romano. grata ea legatio barbaro fuit; collocutusque cum legatis de ratione belli gerendi, ut veterum militum verba audivit, quam multarum rerum ipse ignarus esset animadvertit. tum oravit ut duo legationem referrent ad imperatores suos, unus apud sese magister rei militaris restaret: rudem ad pedestria bella **Numidarum** gentem esse, equis tantum **habilem**; sed habere hostem pedestri fidentem **Marti**, cui si **aequari** velit, et sibi pedites comparandos esse. facturos se in praesentia quod vellet legati respondent, fide accepta ut remitteret extemplo eum, si imperatores sui non comprobassent factum. Q. Statorio nomen fuit, qui ad regem remansit.

Livy XXIV.48

Words
miserunt: the Scipio brothers are the subject; **habilis** adj = expert; **aequor** 1pass = be equal.
Names
Numida 1m = a Numidian; **Mars Martis** 3m = Mars, god of war: hence = war.

74. A quarrel over a mule leads to the death of a soldier, and soon to a full-scale battle.

On that day neither the consul nor the King wished to fight, but Fortune, which is more powerful than human planning, brought about a battle.

flumen erat haud magnum propius hostium castra, ex quo et **Macedones** et Romani aquabantur, praesidiis ex utraque ripa positis ut id facere tuto possent. duae cohortes **a parte** Romanorum erant et duae turmae **Samnitium** equitum, quibus praeerat M.Sergius Silus legatus; et aliud pro castris erat praesidium sub C.Cluvio legato, tres cohortes et duae turmae equitum. cum otium ad flumen esset, neutris lacessentibus, hora circiter nona, **iumentum**, e manibus curantium elapsum, in ulteriorem ripam effugit. quod cum per aquam ferme genus tenus altam tres milites sequerentur, et **Thraces** duo id **iumentum** ex medio alveo in suam ripam trahentes caperent, **hos** persecuti **illi**, altero eorum occiso receptoque iumento, ad stationem suorum se recipiebant. octingentorum **Thracum** praesidium in hostium ripa erat. ex his pauci primo, aegre passi **popularem** in suo conspectu caesum, ad persequendos interfectores fluvium transgressi sunt, dein plures, postremo omnes.

Livy XLIV.40

Words
a parte = on the side of; **iumentum** 2n = pack-animal, mule; **hos** = the Thracians; **illi** = the Romans; **popularis** 3m = fellow-countryman.
Names
Macedones 3mpl = Macedonians; **Samnites** 3mpl = Samnites (who are on the Roman side); **Thraces** 3mpl = Thracians.

75. The consul Marcellus falls into an ambush and is killed by a force of Numidians.

A lookout gave a sign to the Numidians to spring out, all at the same time, from their hiding-places. They all leapt out, shouting, and attacked.

cum in ea valle consules essent ut neque evadere possent in iugum occupatum ab hoste nec receptum, ab tergo circumventi, haberent, extrahi tamen diutius certamen potuisset ni coepta ab **Etruscis** fuga pavorem ceteris iniecisset. non tamen omisere pugnam, deserti ab **Etruscis**, **Fregellani** donec **integri** consules rem sustinebant; sed postquam vulneratos ambo consules, Marcellum etiam transfixum **lancea** prolabentem ex equo moribundum videre, tum et ipsi (perpauci autem supererant) cum Crispino consule, duobus iaculis icto, et Marcello adulescente, saucio et ipso, effugerunt. interfectus A.Manlius tribunus militum, et ex duobus praefectis sociorum **M'**Aulius occisus, L.Arrenius captus: et lictores consulum quinque vivi in hostium potestatem venerunt, ceteri aut interfecti aut cum consule effugerunt; equitum tres et quadraginta aut in proelio aut in fuga ceciderunt, duodeviginti vivi capti.

Livy XXVII.27

Words
integer adj = unharmed; **lancea** 1f = lance.
Names
Etrusci 2mpl = Etruscans; **Fregellani** 2mpl = Fregellans; **M'** = Manius.

76. The flute-players of Rome (who played to accompany sacrifices) are deprived of a traditional privilege, and walk out of Rome in protest. The authorities resort to a trick to get them back.

Another thing happened in this year, which would be too trivial to mention if it did not have some connection with religion.

tibicines, quia prohibiti erant in aede Iovis **vesci**, aegre passi, **Tibur** uno agmine abierunt, adeo ut nemo in urbe esset qui sacrificiis praecineret. eius rei religio tenuit senatum, legatosque **Tibur** miserunt ut **darent operam** ut ii homines Romanis restituerentur. **Tiburtini**, benigne polliciti, primum **accitos** eos in curiam hortati sunt uti reverterentur Romam; postquam perpelli nequibant, consilio haud **abhorrente ab** ingeniis hominum eos aggrediuntur. die festo, alii alios **per speciem** celebrandarum cantu epularum invitant, et vino (cuius avidum ferme genus est) oneratos **sopiunt**, atque ita in plaustra, somno vinctos, coniciunt ac Romam deportant; nec prius sensere quam plaustris in foro relictis plenos **crapulae** eos lux oppressit. tunc concursus populi factus, impetratoque ut manerent, restitutum in aede **vescendi** ius iis qui sacris praecinerent.

Livy IX.30

Words

vescor 3dep = have meals; **operam do** 1 = take steps, make an effort; **accio** 4 = summon; **abhorrens abhorrentis** adj **ab** (+abl) = inappropriate to; **per speciem** = on the pretext; **sopio** 4 = send to sleep; **crapula** 1f = drunkenness, hangover.

Names

Tibur Tiburis 3n = Tivoli; **Tiburtini** 3mpl = the people of Tivoli.

77. Theoxena and her family, under threat from King Philip, are hindered by bad weather in their attempt to escape; they have recourse to the only possible way out.

When she heard the proclamation, Theoxena dared to say that she would kill her children herself rather than let them come into the power of Philip. But her husband Poris said he would take them to Athens, to some faithful friends he had there.

proficiscuntur ab **Thessalonica Aeneam** ad sacrificium. ibi, die per sollemnes epulas consumpto, navem praeparatam a **Poride** de tertia vigilia conscenderunt tamquam redituri **Thessalonicam**; sed traicere in **Euboeam** erat propositum. ceterum in adversum ventum nequiquam eos tendentes prope terram lux oppressit, et **regii lembum** armatum ad retrahendam eam navem miserunt, cum gravi **edicto** ne reverterentur sine ea. cum iam appropinquabant, **Poris** quidem ad hortationem **remigum** nautarumque intentus erat; interdum, manus ad caelum tendens, deos ut ferrent opem orabat. ferox interim femina venenum **diluit** ferrumque **promit** et, posito in conspectu poculo, strictisque gladiis, "mors," inquit, "una **vindicta** est. viae ad mortem hae sunt. agite, iuvenes mei: capite ferrum, aut haurite poculum si segnior mors iuvat." et hostes aderant et auctor mortis instabat: alii alio leto absumpti semianimes e nave praecipitantur. ipsa deinde virum, comitem mortis, complexa, in mare sese deiecit.

Livy XL.4

Words
regii 2mpl = the king's men; **lembus** 2m = boat; **edictum** 2n = command; **remex remigis** 3m = rower; **diluo** 3 = mix; **promo** 3 = take out; **vindicta** 1f = escape.

Names
Thessalonica 1f, **Aenea** 1f, and **Euboea** 1f are all places in Greece; **Poris Poridis** 3m = Poris.

78. Hannibal is encamped outside the gates of Rome. After bad weather stops battle, various occurrences suggest that he will not capture the city, but he makes an appropriate response to one of them.

Because outbreaks of panic kept flaring up in the city, it was decided that all who had been dictators or censors or consuls should be invested with official authority until the enemy had moved away from the walls. During the rest of that day and night there were various further outbreaks, but these were suppressed.

postero die, transgressus **Anienem**, Hannibal in aciem omnes copias eduxit; nec Flaccus consulesque certamen **detrectavere**. instructis utrimque exercitibus, imber ingens grandine mixtus ita utramque aciem turbavit ut, vix armis retentis, in castra sese receperint. et postero die eodem loco acies instructas **eadem** tempestas diremit; ubi recepissent se in casta, mira serenitas cum tranquillitate oriebatur. **in religionem** ea res apud **Poenos** versa est. minuere etiam spem eius duae aliae, parva magnaque res: magna illa quod, cum ipse ad moenia urbis Romanae armatus sederet, milites **in supplementum Hispaniae** profectos audiit; parva autem quod per eos dies eum forte agrum in quo ipse castra haberet **venisse**, nihil ob id deminuto pretio, cognitum ex quodam captivo est. (id vero adeo superbum atque indignum visum ut extemplo, vocato **praecone**, **tabernas argentarias** quae circum Forum Romanum essent iusserit **venire**.) his motus, ad **Tutiam** fluvium castra rettulit, sex milia passuum ab urbe.

Livy XXVI.11

Words

detrecto 1 = decline, refuse; **eadem** = the same sort of; **in religionem** = as an omen; **in supplementum** = as reinforcements; **veneo venire veni** = be sold; **praeco praeconis** 3m = auctioneer; **taberna argentaria** 1f = bank.

Names

Anio Anienis 3m = the river Anio; **Poeni** 2mpl = the Carthaginians; **Hispania 1f** = Spain; **Tutia** 1f = the river Tutia.

79. Some rather naive ambassadors are allowed by the praetor Gracchus to go and ask for military assistance against him; but his army proves too impressive for the prospective reinforcements.

He first took Munda, attacking it unexpectedly by night. He took hostages, and left a garrison there. Then he captured castles and burned the countryside until he reached another strong city, which the Celts call Certima.

ubi cum iam **opera** admoveret, veniunt legati ex oppido, quorum sermo antiquae simplicitatis fuit, non **dissimulantium** bellaturos, si vires essent. petierunt enim ut sibi in castra **Celtiberorum** ire liceret ad auxilia accienda: si non impetrasset, tum separatim ab illis consulturos. permittente Graccho, ierunt, et post paucis diebus alios decem legatos secum adduxerunt. meridianum tempus erat. nihil prius petierunt a praetore quam ut bibere sibi iubet dari. epotis primis poculis, iterum poposcerunt, magno risu circumstantium in tam rudibus ingeniis. tum **maximus natu** ex illis "missi sumus," inquit, "a gente nostra qui **sciscitaremur** qua re fretus arma nobis inferres." ad hanc **percontationem** Gracchus exercitu se egregio fidentem venisse respondit; quem si ipsi videre velint, quo certiora ad suos referant, potestatem se eis facturum esse. tribunis militum imperat ut ornari omnes copias peditum equitumque iubeant. ab hoc spectaculo legati, dimissi, deterruerunt suos ab auxilio circumsessae urbi ferendo. oppidani, destituti ab unica spe auxilii, in deditionem venerunt.

Livy XL.47

Words

opera 3npl = siege machines; **dissimulo** 1 = pretend...not; **maximus natu** = oldest; **sciscitor** 1dep = ask; **percontatio percontationis** 3f = enquiry.

Names

Celtiberi 2mpl = the Celtiberians, a Spanish tribe.

80. When two Roman armies are trapped in a mountain pass (the "Caudine Forks") by the Samnites, a retired Samnite statesman is consulted about what to do with them. The Samnites do not understand his replies and summon him to explain.

The Samnites did not know what to do with such a stroke of luck, so they wrote to Herennius Pontius, the father of their general, to see what he thought.

iam is, gravatus annis, non militaribus solum sed civilibus quoque abscesserat **muneribus**; in corpore tamen **affecto vigebat** vis animi consiliique. is ubi accepit ad **Furculas Caudinas** inter duos saltus clausos esse exercitus Romanos, consultus ab nuntio filii, censuit omnes inde quam primum inviolatos dimittendos. quae ubi spreta sententia est iterumque consulebatur, censuit ad unum omnes interficiendos. quae ubi tam **discordia** inter se responsa data sunt, quamquam filius ipse in primis iam animum quoque **consenuisse** in **affecto** corpore rebatur, tamen consensu omnium victus est ut ipsum in consilium **acciret**. senex plaustro in castra dicitur advectus, vocatusque in consilium ita ferme locutus esse ut nihil sententiae suae mutaret, causas tantum adiceret: priore se consilio, quod optimum duceret, cum potentissimo populo per ingens beneficium perpetuam firmare pacem amicitiamque; altero consilio in multas aetates quibus, amissis duobus exercitibus, haud facile receptura vires res Romana esset, bellum **differre**; tertium nullum consilium esse.

Livy IX.3

Words
munus muneris 3n (here) = office; **affectus** adj = ailing; **vigeo** 2 = be strong; **discors discordis** adj = differing; **consenesco** 3 **consenui** = go senile; **accio** 4 = summon; **differo differre** = avert, put off.
Names
Furculae Caudinae 1fpl = the Caudine Forks.

80

81. There are plenty of precedents for wars over women: Ovid has won his, but without bloodshed.

No one else has done my fighting for me, as happened at Troy: I've won my war under my own generalship, and I've been my own army, my own cavalryman, my own infantry, my own standard-bearer.

nec belli est nova causa mei: nisi rapta fuisset
  Tyndaris, Europae pax Asiaeque foret.
femina silvestres **Lapithas populum**que **biformem**
  turpiter **apposito** vertit in arma **mero**;
femina Troianos iterum nova bella movere
  impulit in regno, iuste **Latine**, tuo;
femina Romanis, **etiamnunc urbe recenti**,
  inmisit soceros armaque saeva dedit.
vidi ego pro nivea pugnantes coniuge tauros:
  spectatrix animos ipsa iuvenca dabat.
me quoque, qui multos, sed me sine caede, **Cupido**
  iussit militiae signa movere suae.
                   Ovid, Amores II.12

Words

apposito mero = when the wine was served; **etiamnunc...recenti**: i.e. in the early days of Rome, when the Romans caused a war with the Sabines by carrying off some of their women; **inmitto 3 inmisi** = send [someone] to war against (+dat); **socer soceri** 2m = father-in-law.

Names

Tyndaris Tyndaridis 3f = Helen; **Lapithae** 1mpl = the Lapiths, who got into a bloody fight with the Centaurs (**populus biformis**) at a wedding feast; **Latinus** 2m = Latinus, an Italian king for whose daughter Aeneas the Trojan and Turnus fought; **Cupido Cupidinis** 3m = Cupid.

82. In general, girls would rather be given presents than poems: though there are a few cultured ones (or ones who think they are) who may take some small pleasure in your poems.

You must, of course, give your girlfriend gifts: small ones sometimes, perhaps, but carefully chosen; send her fruit and say it came from your estate; send her a dove, or a thrush.

quid tibi praecipiam teneros quoque mittere versus?
  ei mihi, non multum carmen honoris habet!
carmina laudantur, sed munera magna petuntur:
  dummodo sit dives, barbarus ipse placet.
aurea sunt vere nunc **saecula**: plurimus auro
  venit honos; auro **conciliatur** amor.
ipse licet venias, **Musis** comitatus, **Homere**,
  si nihil attuleris, **ibis**, **Homere**, **foras**.
sunt tamen et doctae (rarissima turba) puellae;
  altera non doctae turba, sed esse volunt.
utraque laudetur per carmina; carmina **lector**
  commendet dulci **qualiacumque** sono;
his ergo aut illis **vigilatum** carmen in ipsas
  forsitan exigui muneris **instar** erit.
Ovid, The Art of Love II. 273

Words

aurea saecula: there is a pun on the idea of the "Golden Age"; **concilio** 1 (here) = buy, gain; **eo (ire** etc) **foras** = go away; **lector commendet** = "let the reader (i.e. you) improve..."; **qualiacumque** = "whatever they're like"; **vigilatum** = "that you've spent all night over"; **instar** (+gen) = equivalent to.

Names

Musae 1fpl = the Muses, goddesses of poetry and the arts; **Homerus** 2m = the poet Homer.

83. Lovers are like soldiers: they endure the same kind of hardships, but with different aims.

Every lover is a soldier: Cupid has his army too. The age for fighting is the age for love...soldier and lover both stay awake all night, one outside his general's tent, the other outside his girlfriend's door; travel is part of a soldier's life, and if you send the lover's girl away, he'll go anywhere after her.

quis nisi vel miles vel amans et frigora noctis
  et denso mixtas perferet imbre nives?
mittitur infestos alter **speculator** in hostes;
  in rivale oculos alter, ut hoste, tenet.
ille graves urbes, hic durae limen amicae
  obsidet; hic portas frangit, at ille fores.
saepe **soporatos** invadere **profuit** hostes,
  caedere et armata vulgus inerme manu;
sic fera **Threicii** ceciderunt agmina **Rhesi**,
  et dominum, capti, deseruistis, equi:
nempe maritorum somnis utuntur amantes
  et sua **sopitis** hostibus arma movent.
ergo **desidiam** quicumque vocabat amorem,
  desinat: **ingenii** est **experientis** amor.

                     Ovid, Amores I.9

Words

speculator speculatoris 3m = spy; **soporatus** adj = sleeping; **profuit (prosum)** = it has been useful; **sopitus** adj = sleeping; **desidia** 1f = idleness; **ingenii experientis** = "for a character prepared to try anything."

Names

Threicius Rhesus 2m = Rhesus, king of Thrace, who was killed at Troy while asleep, and his famous horses captured.

83

84. Cupid (Amor) is worried about Ovid's new book, the "Cure for Love". Ovid reassures him that he has no hostile intent: he, Ovid, will always be a lover; the book is for those who are not so inclined.

[The passage is the beginning of the poem, which is a sequel to the "Art of Love", for those whose love affairs have turned out unhappy.]

legerat huius Amor titulum nomenque **libelli**:
  "bella mihi, video, bella parantur!" ait.
parce tuum vatem sceleris damnare, Cupido,
  tradita qui toties, te duce, **signa tuli**!
non ego **Tydides**, a quo tua saucia mater
  in liquidum rediit aethera **Martis** equis.
saepe tepent alii iuvenes; ego semper amavi,
  et si quid faciam nunc quoque quaeris, amo.
nec te, **blande** puer, nec nostras prodimus artes,
  nec nova praeteritum **Musa retexit** opus.
si quis amat quod amare iuvat, feliciter ardens
  gaudeat, et vento naviget ille suo;
at si quis male fert indignae regna puellae,
  ne pereat, nostrae sentiat artis opem.
Ovid, The Cure for Love 1

Words
libellus 2m = little book; **tradita...signa tuli** = "I who have carried the standards entrusted to me..."; **blandus** adj = charming; **retexo** 3 = reverse, rewrite.
Names
Tydides Tydidis 3m = Diomedes, son of Tydeus, who wounded Venus during the Trojan War; **Mars Martis** 3m = Mars, god of war and lover of Venus; **Musa** 1f = a Muse, a goddess of poetry, in this case Ovid's own poetic inspiration.

85. Desperate to stop Ulysses sailing away, Calypso keeps asking him to tell her stories about the Trojan War. This particular one comes to an abrupt end.

Don't forget that a handsome young man will end up grey and wrinkly: build up your character and cultivate your mind so that you're interesting as well as good-looking.

non formosus erat, sed erat facundus Ulixes,
  et tamen aequoreas torsit amore deas.
a! quotiens illum doluit properare Calypso,
  remigioque aptas esse negavit aquas!
haec Troiae casus iterumque iterumque rogabat;
  ille referre aliter saepe solebat idem.
litore constiterant: illic quoque pulchra Calypso
  exigit Odrysii fata cruenta ducis.
ille levi virga (virgam nam forte tenebat)
  quod rogat in **spisso** litore pingit opus;
"haec," inquit, "Troia est" (muros in litore fecit);
  "hic tibi sit **Simois**: haec mea castra puta;
illic **Sithonii** fuerant tentoria **Rhesi**;
  hac ego sum captis nocte revectus equis..."
pluraque pingebat, subitus cum **Pergama** fluctus
  abstulit et **Rhesi** cum duce castra suo.
Ovid, The Art of Love II.123

Words
remigium 2n = rowing; **exigo** 3 = ask about; **spissus** adj = dense, sandy.

Names
Odrysius adj and **Sithonius** adj both = Thracian; **Simois Simoentis** 3m = the river Simois, near Troy; **Rhesus** 2m = Rhesus, king of Thrace, whom Ulysses killed at Troy and whose horses he captured; **Pergama** 2npl = Pergama, the stronghold of Troy.

86. Love is more important than money: Tibullus hopes for his girlfriend's safe return from a journey.

What's the good of houses with marble columns and purple cushions and all the things most people want? They only make others jealous: "most people" are quite wrong in what they want.

non opibus mentes hominum curaeque levantur,
  nam Fortuna sua tempora lege regit.
sit mihi paupertas tecum iucunda, Neaera:
  at sine te regum munera nulla volo.
o **niveam** quae te poterit mihi reddere **lucem**!
  o mihi felicem terque quaterque diem!
at si, pro dulci reditu quaecumque voventur,
  audiat aversa non meus aure deus,
nec me regna iuvant nec **Lydius aurifer amnis**
  nec quas terrarum sustinet orbis opes.
et si fata negant reditum **tristesque sorores**,
  stamina quae ducunt quaeque futura canunt,
me vocet in vastos amnes nigramque paludem
  dives in ignava luridus **Orcus** aqua.
                    Tibullus, III.3

Words

o niveam...lucem = o bright day! (accusative of exclamation); **tristes sorores** = the Fates, who weave the destinies of men; **stamen staminis** 3n = thread.

Names

Lydius...amnis = the river Pactolus in Lydia, to which King Midas transferred his gold-producing powers; **Orcus** 2m = Orcus, the god of the Underworld (who is described as **dives** because everything comes to him in the end).

87. Even a witch like Circe can't make a man love her if he d
want to.

I shan't give you any advice about using herbs and magic in your love
affairs: Circe was a witch, but she couldn't stop Ulysses leaving her,
even though she spoke to him like this:

"non ego, quod primo (memini) sperare solebam,
  iam precor, ut coniunx tu meus esse velis.
et tamen, ut coniunx essem tua, digna videbar,
  quod dea, quod magni filia **Solis** eram.
ne properes oro: spatium pro munere posco;
  quid minus optari per mea vota potest?
et freta mota vides, et debes illa timere:
  utilior velis postmodo ventus erit.
quae tibi causa fugae? non hic nova Troia resurgit,
  non aliquis socios rursus ad arma vocat.
hic amor et pax est, in qua male vulneror una,
  tutaque sub regno terra futura tuo est."
illa loquebatur, navem solvebat Ulixes:
  irrita cum velis verba tulere **Noti**.
ardet et assuetas Circe **decurrit ad** artes,
  nec tamen est illis attenuatus amor.

Ovid, The Cure for Love 273

Words
irritus adj = vain, futile; **decurro** 3 **ad** (+acc) = have recourse to.
Names
Sol Solis 3m = the Sun-god, Circe's father; **Notus** 2m = the South
Wind.

who has already been abandoned by Theseus, Bacchus is now going to desert her too.

...us had returned from his conquest of India, loaded
...s, including a pretty princess who pleased Bacchus only
...oo well.

flebat amans coniunx **spatiata**que litore curvo
  edidit **incultis** talia verba comis:
"en, iterum, fluctus, similes audite querelas!
  en, iterum lacrimas accipe, harena, meas!
dicebam, memini, 'periure et perfide **Theseu**!'
  ille abiit. eadem crimina Bacchus habet.
nunc quoque 'nulla viro', clamabo, 'femina credat!'
  nomine mutato, causa relata mea est:
o utinam mea sors, qua primum coeperat, isset,
  iamque ego praesenti tempore nulla forem.
quid me desertis perituram, **Liber**, harenis
  servabas? potui **dedoluisse** semel.
ausus es, ante oculos adducta **paelice** nostros,
  tam bene compositum sollicitare torum?
heu! ubi **pacta** fides? ubi quae iurare solebas?
  me miseram! quotiens haec ego verba loquar?"
              Ovid, Fasti III.467

Words
spatior 1dep = pace about; **incultus** adj = dishevelled; **o utinam...isset**:
Ariadne means that she wishes she had died earlier, after Theseus left
her; **dedoleo** 2 = put an end to grief; **paelex paelicis** 3f = mistress,
concubine; **pactus** adj = agreed.
Names
Theseus 2m (voc **Theseu**) = Theseus; **Liber Liberi** 2m = Bacchus.

89. At a country festival, Tibullus gives thanks for the good things that have their origins in the countryside, including Cupid (Amor), who is supposed to have first learnt his skills there.

It is the country that bears our harvest, and in the country the bees in springtime fill the combs with honey; country people were the first to sing and play the pipes, and the first to dance.

ipse quoque inter agros interque armenta Cupido
  natus et indomitas dicitur inter equas.
illic indocto primum se exercuit arcu:
  ei mihi! quam doctas nunc habet ille manus!
nec pecudes, velut ante, petit: fixisse puellas
  gestit et audaces perdomuisse viros.
hic iuveni **detraxit** opes, hic dicere iussit
  limen ad iratae verba **pudenda** senem;
hoc duce **custodes** furtim transgressa iacentes
  ad iuvenem tenebris sola puella venit.
a miseri, quos hic graviter deus urget! at ille
  felix, cui placidus leniter adflat Amor.
sancte, veni dapibus festis; sed **pone** sagittas
  et procul ardentes hinc, precor, abde **faces**.

Tibullus II.1

Words

gestio 4 = rejoice; **detraho** 3 **detraxi** = take away; **limen ad** = **ad limen**; **pudendus** adj = shameful; **custodes** = the slaves who should be guarding the door; **pono** 3 (here) = put aside; **fax facis** 3f = torch.

90. Propertius bitterly complains that his girl is leaving him; he may as well die, but even then he will not be free of her vindictiveness.

The girl I have loved so much is being taken from me: and you, my friend, do you tell me not to weep at such a time?

possum ego in alterius positam spectare lacerto?
  nec mea dicetur, quae modo dicta mea est?
omnia vertuntur: certe vertuntur amores;
  vinceris aut vincis - haec in amore **rota** est.
magni saepe duces, magni cecidere tyranni,
  et **Thebae** steterant altaque Troia fuit.
munera quanta dedi vel qualia carmina feci!
  illa tamen numquam, ferrea, dixit "amo."
ergo iam multos nimium temerarius annos,
  improba, qui tulerim teque tuamque domum,
ecquando tibi liber sum visus? an **usque**
  in nostrum iacies verba superba caput?
sic igitur prima **moriere** aetate, Properti?
  sed morere: **interitu** gaudeat illa tuo!
exagitet nostros **manes**, sectetur et umbras,
  insultetque rogis, **calcet** et ossa mea!
                              Propertius II.8

Words
rota 1f = cycle; **ecquando** = ever; **usque** = always; **moriere** = **morieris**; **interitus** 4m = death; **manes manium** 3mpl = ghost; **calco** 1 = trample on.

Names
Thebae 1fpl = Thebes, used, like Troy, to exemplify legendary cities that have vanished.

91. Cicero claims that a conspiracy against the young Sextus Roscius was formed between Titus Roscius, Titus Capito, and Chrysogonus.

While Sextus Roscius was at Ameria and Titus Roscius at Rome, the elder Sextus Roscius was murdered, while returning home from dinner, near the Pallacine Baths in Rome. I think, gentlemen, that from what follows it will be clear on whom suspicion for the crime must fall.

occiso Sex.Roscio, primus Ameriam nuntiat Glaucia, cliens et familiaris istius T.Rosci, et nuntiat domum non fili, sed T.Capitonis inimici; et cum post horam primam noctis occisus esset, **primo diluculo** nuntius hic Ameriam venit. decem horis nocturnis sex et quinquaginta milia passuum pervolavit, non modo ut exoptatum inimico nuntium primus adferret, sed etiam cruorem inimici quam recentissimum telumque paulo ante e corpore extractum ostenderet. **quadriduo quo** haec gesta sunt, res ad Chrysogonum defertur; magnitudo pecuniae demonstratur; bonitas **praediorum** (nam fundos decem et tres reliquit qui fere omnes **Tiberim** tangunt), huius inopia et solitudo commemoratur; demonstrant, cum pater huiusce, Sex.Roscius, homo tam splendidus et gratiosus, nullo negotio sit occisus, perfacile hunc hominem incautum et rusticum et Romae ignotum **de medio tolli** posse; ad eam rem operam suam pollicentur. ne diutius teneam, iudices, societas coitur.

Cicero, For Sextus Roscius 19

Words
primo diluculo = at dawn; **quadriduo quo** = on the fourth day after; **praedium** 2n = estate; **de medio tollo tollere** = get rid of.
Names
Tiberis Tiberis 3m = the river Tiber

92. Cicero describes how he arranged for the arrest of some envoys from the Allobroges (from Gaul), along with one of Catiline's conspirators with whom they had been plotting.

I discovered that Lentulus had plotted with these Allobroges, that they were going to visit Catiline on their way back to Gaul, and that Titus Volturcius was with them carrying a letter to Catiline.

itaque **hesterno die** L.Flaccum et C.Pomptinum, praetores, fortissimos atque amantissimos rei publicae viros, ad me vocavi, rem exposui, quid fieri placeret ostendi. illi autem sine ulla mora negotium susceperunt et, cum **advesperasceret**, occulte ad **Pontem Mulvium** pervenerunt, atque ibi in proximis villis ita **bipertito** fuerunt ut **Tiberis** inter eos interesset. **eodem** autem et ipsi sine cuiusquam suspicione multos fortes viros eduxerat, et ego complures delectos adulescentes cum gladiis miseram. interim tertia fere vigilia **exacta**, cum iam **Pontem Mulvium**, magno **comitatu**, legati Allobroges ingredi inciperent unaque Volturcius, fit in eos impetus; ducuntur et ab illis gladii et a nostris. res praetoribus erat nota solis, ignorabatur a ceteris. tum, **interventu** Pomptini atque Flacci, pugna quae erat commissa **sedatur**. litterae quaecumque erant in eo **comitatu**, integris **signis**, praetoribus traduntur; ipsi, comprehensi, ad me, cum iam **dilucesceret**, deducuntur.

Cicero, Against Catiline III.5

Words

hesterno die = yesterday; **advesperascit** 3 = evening comes; **bipertito** = in two parts; **eodem** = to the same place; **exigo 3 exegi exactum** = finish; **comitatus** 4m = company; **interventus** 4m = intervention; **sedo** 1 = calm, break up; **signum** 2n (here) = seal; **dilucescit** 3 = it gets light.

Names

Pons Mulvius Pontis Mulvii m = the Mulvian Bridge, over the Tiber; **Tiberis Tiberis** 3m = the river Tiber.

93. Cicero asks Caesar to forgive King Deiotarus for supporting Pompey at the beginning of the Civil War.

Who does not know how great was Pompey's name? He eclipsed his predecessors by as much as you, Caesar, have eclipsed all others. Your wars, victories, triumphs, consulships, we cannot count; but still we used to count with admiration those of Pompey.

ad eum igitur rex Deiotarus venit hoc misero fatalique bello, quem antea iustis hostilibusque bellis adiuverat, quocum erat non hospitio solum verum etiam familiaritate coniunctus, et venit vel rogatus ut amicus, vel arcessitus ut socius, vel evocatus ut is qui senatui parere didicisset: postremo, venit ut ad fugientem, non ut ad insequentem, id est periculi, non ad victoriae, societatem. itaque **Pharsalico proelio** facto a Pompeio discessit, domum se contulit, teque **Alexandrinum bellum** gerente utilitatibus tuis paruit. ille exercitum Cn.Domiti, amplissimi viri, suis tectis et copiis sustentavit; ille **Ephesum**, ad eum quem tu ex tuis fidelissimum et **probatissimum** omnibus delegisti, pecuniam misit; ille corpus suum periculo **obiecit**, tecumque in acie contra **Pharnacem** fuit, tuumque hostem esse **duxit** suum. quae quidem a te in eam partem accepta sunt, Caesar, ut eum amplissimo regis honore et nomine **adfeceris**.

Cicero, For King Deiotarus 13

Words

probatus adj = tested, proven; **obicio** 3 **obieci** = offer, put [something] in the way of; **duco** 3 **duxi** (here) = think; **adficio** 3 **adfeci** = endow.

Names

Pharsalicum proelium = the battle of Pharsalus; **Alexandrinum bellum** = the Alexandrine war; **Ephesus** 2f = Ephesus, a town in Asia Minor; **Pharnaces Pharnacis** 3m = Pharnaces, king of Pontus.

94. How the doctor Strato was revealed to be a thief and a murderer.

Some time afterwards, although she had pretended that she believed that he had poisoned her husband, Sassia presented Strato with a shop so that he could set up a medical practice at Larinum.

hoc ipso fere tempore Strato ille medicus furtum fecit et caedem eius modi. cum esset in aedibus **armarium** in quo sciret esse **nummorum** aliquantum et auri, noctu duos servos dormientes occidit in **piscinam**que deiecit. ipse **armari fundum exsecuit** et **HS X** et **auri quinque pondo** abstulit, uno ex servis (puero non grandi) conscio. furto postridie cognito, omnis suspicio in eos servos qui **non comparebant** commovebatur. cum exsectio illa **fundi** in **armario** animadverteretur, homines quaerebant quonam modo fieri potuisset. quidam ex amicis Sassiae **recordatus est** se nuper in auctione quadam vidisse **aduncam** et **dentatam venire serrulam**, qua illud potuisse ita circumsecari videretur. ne multa, perquiritur a **coactoribus**, invenitur ea **serrula** ad Stratonem pervenisse. hoc initio suspicionis orto, et aperte **insimulato** Stratone, puer ille conscius pertimuit, rem omnem indicavit; homines in **piscina** inventi sunt, Strato in vincula coniectus est, atque etiam in taberna eius **nummi**, nequaquam omnes, reperiuntur.

Cicero, For Cluentius 179

Words

armarium 2n = chest; **nummus** 2m = coin; **piscina** 1f = fishpond; **fundus** 2m = bottom; **exseco** 1 **exsecui** = cut out; **HS X** = 10,000 sesterces; **auri...pondo** = five pounds of gold; **non comparebant** = "could not be found"; **recordor** 1dep = remember; **aduncus** adj = curved; **dentatus** adj = with teeth; **veneo venire veni** = be sold; **serrula** 1f = saw; **coactores** 3mpl = the auctioneers; **insimulo** 1 = accuse;

95. Cicero urges Caesar to leave a lasting memorial to posterity by re-establishing the state on a sound footing after the Civil War.

The life that you must lead now is not one confined by flesh and blood, but one which will live in the memory of those to come: you have achieved many things to be wondered at; you must now achieve things for which you will be praised.

obstupescent posteri certe imperia, provincias, **Rhenum**, **Oceanum**, **Nilum**, pugnas innumerabiles, incredibiles victorias, monumenta, munera, triumphos audientes et legentes tuos. sed nisi haec urbs **stabilita** tuis consiliis et institutis erit, vagabitur modo tuum nomen longe atque late; sedem stabilem et domicilium certum non habebit. erit inter eos etiam qui nascentur, sicut inter nos fuit, magna dissensio, cum alii laudibus ad caelum res gestas efferent, alii fortasse aliquid **requirent**, nisi belli civilis incendium salute patriae **restinxeris**. **servi** igitur eis iudicibus qui, multis post saeculis, de te iudicabunt et quidem incorruptius quam nos; nam et sine amore et sine cupiditate et rursus sine odio et sine invidia iudicabunt. id autem etiam si tum ad te, ut quidam falso putant, non **pertinebit**, nunc certe **pertinet** esse te talem ut tuas laudes obscuratura nulla umquam sit oblivio.

Cicero, For Marcellus 28

Words

stabilio 4 = stabilise; **requiro** 3 = look for, miss; **restinguo** 3 **restinxi** = extinguish; **servi** is imperative of **servio** 4 (+dat) (here) = have regard for; **pertineo** 2 = matter.

Names

Rhenus 2m = the river Rhine; **Oceanus** 2m = the Ocean; **Nilus** 2m = the Nile: the three of them signify Caesar's campaigns in Germany, Britain, and Egypt respectively.

96. Cicero describes the violence used against his brother and his other supporters when they tried to speak in the assembly in favour of Cicero's return from exile.

On the day that my case was to be discussed in the assembly, Sestius, who is accused of using violence, did nothing at all: he waited to see what my enemies would do. And what did they do, those men who have now accused Sestius of violence?

cum forum, comitium, curiam armatis hominibus ac servis plerisque occupavissent, impetum faciunt in Fabricium, manus adferunt, occidunt nonnullos, vulnerant multos. venientem in forum virum optimum et **constantissimum**, M.Cispium, tribunum plebis, vi depellunt. caedem in foro maximam faciunt, universique, destrictis gladiis, in omnibus fori partibus fratrem meum, virum optimum, fortissimum, meique amantissimum, oculis quaerebant, voce poscebant. quorum ille telis libenter, non repugnandi sed moriendi causa, corpus obtulisset suum, nisi **suam vitam ad spem mei reditus reservasset**. subiit tamen vim illam nefariam consceleratorum latronum et, cum ad fratris salutem a populo Romano **deprecandam** venisset, pulsus e rostris in comitio iacuit, vitamque tum suam noctis et fugae praesidio, non iuris iudiciorumque, defendit. meministis tum, iudices, corporibus civium **Tiberim** compleri, **cloacas refarciri**, e foro **effingi spongiis** sanguinem.

Cicero, For Sestius 75

Words
constans constantis adj = steadfast; **suam...reservasset** = "[he] had devoted his life to the hope of my return"; **deprecor** 1dep = beg for; **cloaca** 1f = sewer; **refarcio** 4 = block; **effingo** 3 = mop up; **spongia** 1f = sponge.
Names
Tiberis Tiberis 3m = the river Tiber.

97. Cicero suggests that the jury ignore the evidence that will be given by some Gauls against Fonteius: how can one trust the oaths of such an irreligious people, who even go so far as to practise human sacrifice?

Other nations undertake wars for the sake of their religion: these Gauls wage war against all religions; others, in waging war, seek peace and forgiveness from the gods: they wage war even against the gods themselves.

hae sunt nationes quae quondam, tam longe a suis sedibus, **Delphos** usque ad **Apollinem Pythium** atque ad oraculum vexandum ac spoliandum profectae sunt. ab isdem gentibus sanctis et in testimonio religiosis obsessum **Capitolium** est, atque ille **Iuppiter** cuius nomine maiores nostri vinctum testimonium esse voluerunt. postremo his quicquam sanctum ac religiosum videri potest qui, si **quando**, aliquo metu adducti, deos placandos esse arbitrantur, humanis hostiis eorum aras ac templa **funestant**, ut ne religionem quidem colere possint nisi eam ipsam prius scelere violarint? quis enim ignorat eos usque ad hanc diem retinere illam immanem ac barbaram consuetudinem hominum **immolandorum**? quam ob rem quali fide, quali pietate existimatis esse eos qui etiam deos immortales arbitrentur hominum scelere et sanguine facillime posse placari? cum his vos testibus vestram religionem coniungetis, ab his quicquam sancte aut moderate dictum putabitis?

Cicero, For Fonteius 30

Words
quando = ever; **funesto** 1 = defile; **immolo** 1 = sacrifice.
Names
Delphi 2mpl = Delphi, in Greece, site of the famous oracle; **Apollo Pythius** = Pythian Apollo, the god who was supposed to inspire the responses of the oracle; **Capitolium** 2n = the Capitoline Hill at Rome; **Iuppiter** (here) = the Temple of Jupiter.

98. Sestius, though a tribune and thus technically inviolable, was beaten up by Clodius' gang and left for dead: yet he is now being accused of violence!

And yet not even after this did Sestius have recourse to using the protection of his friends while carrying out his duties as a tribune.

itaque, fretus sanctitate **tribunatus**, cum se non modo contra vim et ferrum sed etiam contra verba atque **interfationem** legibus sacratis esse armatum putaret, venit in templum Castoris, **obnuntiavit** consuli: cum subito manus illa Clodiana exclamat, incitatur, invadit; inermem atque imparatum tribunum alii gladiis adoriuntur, alii fragmentis **saeptorum** et **fustibus**; a quibus hic, multis vulneribus acceptis ac debilitato corpore et contrucidato, se abiecit exanimatus, neque ulla re ab se mortem nisi opinione mortis depulit. quem cum iacentem et concisum plurimis vulneribus viderent, **defatigatione** magis et errore quam misericordia et **modo**, aliquando caedere destiterunt. et causam dicit Sestius de vi? quid ita? quia vivit. at id non sua culpa: **plaga** una illa extrema defuit, quae si accessisset, reliquum spiritum exhausisset. accusa **Lentidium**: non percussit locum! **male dic Titio**, cum tam temere exclamaverit occisum! ipsum vero quid accusas? num **defuit** gladiis? num repugnavit? num, ut gladiatoribus imperari solet, **ferrum non recepit**?

Cicero, For Sestius 79

Words

tribunatus 4m = the tribunate, office of tribune; **interfatio interfationis** 3f = interruption; **obnuntio** 1 = announce unfavourable omens; **saeptum** 2n = fence; **fustis fustis** 3m = club; **defatigatio defatigationis** 3f = exhaustion; **modus** 2m (here) = moderation; **plaga** 1f = blow; **male dico** 3 (+ dat) = abuse, criticise; **desum deesse defui** (+dat) (here) = avoid; **ferrum recipio** 3 **recepi** = "receive the fatal blow", as defeated gladiators were ordered to do.

Names

Lentidius 2m and **Titius** 2m are two members of Clodius's gang.

99. Cicero says that the unanimity of the citizens against Antony is encouraging him in this time of extreme crisis.

So, citizens, I shall stand sentry for you, I shall keep watch for you, with whatever counsel I can, with whatever labour I can employ.

etenim quis est civis tam immemor patriae, tam inimicus dignitati suae, quem non excitet, non inflammet, tantus vester iste consensus? multas magnasque habui consul contiones, multis interfui: nullam umquam vidi tantam quanta nunc vestra est. unum sentitis omnes, unum studetis: M.Antoni **conatus** avertere a re publica, furorem exstinguere, opprimere audaciam. idem volunt omnes ordines; **eodem incumbunt municipia, coloniae,** cuncta Italia. itaque senatum, bene sua sponte firmum, firmiorem vestra auctoritate fecistis. venit tempus, **Quirites,** serius omnino quam dignum populo Romano fuit, sed tamen ita **maturum** ut differri iam hora non possit. populum Romanum servire non fas est, quem di immortales omnibus gentibus imperare voluerunt. res in extremum est adducta discrimen: de libertate decernitur. aut vincatis oportet, **Quirites,** quod profecto et pietate vestra et tanta concordia consequemini, aut quidvis potius quam serviatis. aliae nationes servitutem pati possunt: populi Romani est propria libertas.

Cicero, Philippic VI.18

Words
conatus 4m = attempt, plot; **eodem** = "to that same purpose"; **incumbo** 3 (+dat) (here) = devote oneself; **municipium** 2m = provincial town; **colonia** 1f = colony; **maturus** adj = ripe.

Names
Quirites Quiritium 3mpl = [Roman] citizens.

100. The example of great men who have been exiled or suffered should teach us to prefer long-term reputation to short-term advantage.

Those Greek men whom I have mentioned who were unjustly condemned and exiled by their fellow-countrymen are now famous not only in Greece but all over the world, yet no one remembers the men who drove them into exile.

quis **Carthaginiensium pluris** fuit **Hannibale**, consilio, virtute, rebus gestis, qui unus cum tot imperatoribus nostris per tot annos de imperio et de gloria decertavit? hunc sui cives e civitate eiecerunt: nos etiam hostem litteris nostris et memoria videmus esse celebratum. qua re imitemur nostros Brutos, Camillos, Scipiones, innumerabiles alios qui hanc rem publicam stabiliverunt; quos equidem in deorum immortalium **coetu** et numero repono. amemus patriam, pareamus senatui, consulamus bonis; praesentes fructus neglegamus, posteritatis gloriae serviamus; id esse optimum putemus quod erit rectissimum; speremus quae volumus, sed quod acciderit feramus; cogitemus denique corpus virorum fortium magnorumque hominum esse mortale, **animi** vero **motus** et virtutis gloriam **sempiternam**; neque, hanc opinionem si in illo sanctissimo **Hercule consecratam** videmus, cuius corpore **ambusto** vitam eius et virtutem immortalitas excepisse dicatur, minus existimemus eos qui hanc tantam rem publicam suis consiliis aut laboribus aut auxerint aut defenderint aut servarint esse immortalem gloriam consecutos.

Cicero, For Sestius 142

Words

pluris = worth more, of more importance; **coetus** 4m = company; **animi motus** 4mpl = operations/activities of the mind; **sempiternus** adj = eternal; **consecro** 1 (here) = confirm; **amburo 3 ambussi ambustum** = burn.

Names

Carthaginienses Carthaginiensium 3mpl = the Carthaginians; **Hannibal Hannibalis** 3m = Hannibal; **Hercules Herculis** 3m = Hercules, whose mortal body was cremated, though he himself became a god.

101. **Persephone has been carried off by Dis, the god of the Underworld; her mother, the goddess Ceres, finds the first evidence of what has happened to her.**

It would take a long time to enumerate the lands and seas that Ceres crossed in her search; eventually there was nowhere she had not been.

Sicaniam repetit, dumque omnia lustrat eundo,
venit et ad **Cyanen**; ea, ni mutata fuisset,
omnia narrasset, sed et os et lingua volenti
dicere non aderant, nec qua loqueretur habebat;
signa tamen manifesta dedit, notamque parenti
Persephones zonam summis ostendit in undis.
quam simul agnovit, tamquam tunc denique raptam
scisset, inornatos **laniavit** diva capillos
et **repetita** suis percussit pectora palmis.
nescit adhuc ubi sit; terras tamen **increpat** omnes
ingratasque vocat nec frugum munere dignas,
Trinacriam ante alias, in qua vestigia **damni**
repperit.

Ovid, Metamorphoses V.464

Words
zona 1f = belt; **lanio** 1 = tear; **repetita**: translate as adv = repeatedly;
increpo 1 = curse; **damnum** 2n = loss.
Names
Sicania 1f = Sicily; **Cyane** (acc **Cyanen**) f = Cyane, formerly a nymph,
now a river; **Persephone** (gen **Persephones**) f = Persephone; **Trinacria**
1f = Sicily.

102. Cadmus follows the oracle's instructions and finds a place to found his city.

The oracle said, "You will see a cow in the fields which has never borne the yoke of servitude: follow it, and wherever it first lies down, that will be the place to build your city."

vix bene **Castalio** Cadmus descenderat **antro**,
incustoditam lente videt ire iuvencam
nullum servitii signum cervice gerentem.
subsequitur, **pressoque legit** vestigia **gressu**;
iam vada **Cephisi Panopes**que evaserat arva:
bos stetit et, tollens **speciosam** cornibus altis
ad caelum frontem, **mugitibus** impulit auras
atque ita, respiciens comites sua terga sequentes,
procubuit teneraque latus submisit in herba.
Cadmus agit grates **peregrinae**que oscula terrae
figit et ignotos montes agrosque salutat.
sacra Iovi facturus erat: iubet ire ministros
et petere e silvis **libandas** fontibus undas.

Ovid, Metamorphoses III.14

Words

presso ... gressu = "keeping close behind"; **lego** 3 (here) = follow, track; **speciosus** adj = beautiful, fine; **mugitus** 4m = mooing; **peregrinus** adj = foreign; **libo** 1 = pour as a libation.

Names

Castalium antrum 2n = the cave of the oracle at Delphi; **Cephisus** 2m = the river Cephisus; **Panope** (gen **Panopes**) f = Panope, a town in Greece.

103. The god Morpheus appears to Alcyone in the guise of her drowned husband Ceyx, and tells her what has happened to Ceyx.

Morpheus flew down, assumed the form of Ceyx, and stood before Alcyone's bed; his hair was wet with sea water, and water dripped from his beard.

tum, lecto incumbens, fletu super ora profuso,
haec ait: "agnoscis **Ceyca**, miserrima coniunx?
an mea mutata est facies **nece**? respice: nosces
inveniesque, tuo pro coniuge, coniugis umbram.
nil opis, Alcyone, nobis tua vota tulerunt:
occidimus. falso tibi me promittere noli.
nubilus **Aegaeo** deprendit in aequore navem
Auster et, ingenti iactatam flamine, **solvit**
oraque nostra, tuum frustra clamantia nomen,
implerunt fluctus. non haec tibi nuntiat auctor
ambiguus, non ista vagis rumoribus audis:
ipse ego fata tibi praesens mea **naufragus edo**.
surge, age, da lacrimas, **lugubria**que indue, nec me
indeploratum sub inania **Tartara** mitte".

Ovid, Metamorphoses XI.657

Words

nex necis 3f = death; **solvo** 3 (here) = break up, destroy; **naufragus** adj = shipwrecked; **edo** 3 = explain; **lugubria** 3npl = mourning dress.

Names

Ceyx (acc **Ceyca**) m = Ceyx; **Aegaeus** adj = Aegean; **Auster Austri** 2m = South Wind; **Tartara** 2npl = Tartarus, the Underworld.

104. The peaceful and easy existence of people in the Golden Age.

Either the Creator made man from divine seed, or it was Prometheus who moulded earth and water into creatures that looked like the gods. And man, unlike the other animals, was made to stand upright and look upwards to the heavens.

aurea prima sata est aetas, quae **vindice** nullo,
sponte sua, sine lege, fidem rectumque colebat.
nondum praecipites cingebant oppida fossae;
non galeae, non ensis erat: sine militis usu
mollia securae **peragebant** otia gentes.
ipsa quoque immunis **rastro**que intacta nec ullis
saucia **vomeribus** per se dabat omnia tellus.
ver erat aeternum, placidique tepentibus auris
mulcebant **Zephyri** natos sine semine flores.
mox etiam fruges tellus inarata ferebat,
nec renovatus ager gravidis **canebat aristis**.
flumina iam lactis, iam flumina nectaris ibant,
flavaque de viridi stillabant **ilice** mella.

Ovid, Metamorphoses I.89

Words
vindex vindicis 3m = avenger, protector; **perago** 3 (here) = enjoy; **rastrum** 2n = hoe; **vomer vomeris** 3m = plough; **caneo** 2 = be grey/white; **arista** 1f = ear of corn; **ilex ilicis** 3f = oak.
Names
Zephyrus 2m = West Wind.

105. In remorse at causing the death of Hesperie through a snake bite, Aesacus the Trojan throws himself off a cliff and is changed into a sea-bird.

When the nymph saw Aesacus, she fled like a deer that has seen a wolf, or a duck that has strayed from her lake and been spotted by a hawk:

            quam Troius heros
insequitur, celeremque metu celer urget amore.
ecce! latens herba **coluber** fugientis **adunco**
dente pedem **strinxit, virus**que in corpore liquit.
cum vita suppressa fuga est: amplectitur amens
exanimem clamatque **"piget, piget** esse secutum!
sed non hoc timui, neque erat mihi vincere **tanti**.
perdidimus miseram nos te duo: vulnus ab angue,
a me causa data est. ego sum sceleratior illo,
qui tibi morte mea mortis solacia mittam,"
dixit, et e scopulo, quem rauca subederat unda,
se dedit in pontum; **Tethys**, miserata, cadentem
molliter excepit, nantemque per aequora pennis
texit, et optatae non est data **copia** mortis.
           Ovid, Metamorphoses XI.771

Words
coluber colubri 2m = snake; **aduncus** adj = curved; **stringo** 3 **strinxi** (here) = wound; **virus** 2n = poison; **piget** 2 impers = [I] regret; **tanti** = worth so much; **copia** 1f (here) = opportunity.
Names
Tethys f = Tethys, a sea-goddess.

106. With Neptune's help, Jupiter floods the Earth to punish mankind.

Jupiter's anger was not confined to the heavens, but his brother Neptune helped him with his watery forces: he called the river gods together and said, "There is no need for a long speech from me:

             vires effundite vestras;
sic opus est; aperite domos ac **mole** remota
fluminibus vestris totas **inmittite habenas**."
iusserat. hi redeunt ac fontibus ora relaxant,
et **defrenato** volvuntur in aequora cursu.
ipse tridente suo terram percussit, et illa
intremuit motuque vias patefecit aquarum.
exspatiata ruunt per apertos flumina campos,
cumque satis **arbusta** simul pecudesque virosque
tectaque cumque suis rapiunt **penetralia** sacris.
si qua domus mansit potuitque resistere tanto
indeiecta malo, **culmen** tamen altior huius
unda tegit, pressaeque latent sub gurgite turres;
iamque mare et tellus nullum discrimen habebant:
omnia pontus erant, deerant quoque litora ponto.
              Ovid, Metamorphoses I.278

Words
moles molis 3f (here) = dam (translate as plural); **inmitto habenas** = give rein; **defrenatus** adj = unbridled; **exspatiatus** adj = spreading out; **arbusta** 2npl = plantations; **penetralia** 3npl = shrines; **culmen culminis** 3n = rooftop.

107. The witch Circe (Titania), enraged that Picus will not give up his girlfriend Canens for her, turns him into a woodpecker.

"By your eyes which have captivated me, by your beauty, handsomest of men, accept my love. Accept the all-seeing Sun-god as your father-in-law, and do not cruelly disdain his daughter Circe,"

dixerat; ille ferox ipsamque precesque relinquit,
et "quaecumque es," ait, "non sum tuus. altera captum
me tenet et teneat per longum, comprecor, aevum."
saepe retemptatis precibus Titania frustra,
"non **impune feres** neque," ait, "**reddere Canenti**!"
tum bis ad occasum, bis se convertit ad ortus,
ter iuvenem **baculo** tetigit, tria carmina dixit.
ille fugit, sed se **solito** velocius ipse
currere miratur; pennas in corpore vidit
seque novam subito **Latiis** accedere silvis
indignatus avem, duro fera **robora rostro**
figit et iratus longis dat vulnera ramis.
purpureum **chlamydis** pennae traxere colorem,
nec quicquam antiquum Pico nisi nomina restant.
                    Ovid, Metamorphoses XIV.377

Words
impune fero = get away with [this]; **reddere** = "[you will] be restored";
baculum 2n = stick, magic wand; **solito** = than usual; **se...indignatus** =
"indignant that he..."; **robur roboris** 3n = oak; **rostrum** 2n = beak;
chlamys chlamydis 3f = cloak.
Names
Canens Canentis 3f = Canens; **Latius** adj = of Latium.

108. After repeated warnings from Hercules, Myscelus defies the laws of his city and plans to move away. When brought to trial, he appeals to the god.

Alemon of Argos had one son, who was most beloved by the gods. One night, as he lay asleep, Hercules appeared to him and said, "Go, leave your native land! Seek the waters of the Aesar!"

post ea, discedunt pariter somnusque deusque.
surgit **Alemonides** tacitaque recentia mente
visa refert, pugnatque diu sententia secum:
numen abire iubet, prohibent discedere leges,
poenaque mors posita est patriam mutare volenti.
candidus Oceano nitidum caput abdiderat sol,
et caput extulerat densissima sidereum nox:
visus adesse idem deus est, eademque monere,
et, nisi paruerit, plura et graviora minari.
pertimuit, **patrium**que simul transferre parabat
in sedes **penetrale** novas: fit murmur in urbe,
spretarumque **agitur** legum **reus**; utque peracta est
causa prior crimenque patet sine teste probatum,
squalidus ad superos tollens reus ora manusque,
"o cuius caelum bis sex fecere labores,
fer, precor," inquit "opem! nam tu mihi criminis auctor."
                    Ovid, Metamorphoses XV.25

Words
patrium penetrale n = the shrine of [his] ancestral gods; **reus agor**
3pass = be put on trial; **causa prior** f = the case for the prosecution; **o
cuius...labores** = "you whose twelve labours made you into a god"
(Hercules).
Names
Alemonides Alemonidis 3m = Myscelus, son of Alemon.

109. In the debate as to whether he or Ajax should be awarded the arms of Achilles, Ulysses explains why his skills have been more important to the Greeks' cause in the Trojan War.

I was the one sent as an ambassador to Troy, who dared to enter the Trojan council-chamber, and I fearlessly put our case as I had been instructed:

accusoque Parim, praedamque Helenamque reposco,
et moveo **Priamum Priamo**que **Antenora** iunctum;
at Paris et fratres et qui rapuere sub illo
vix tenuere manus (scis hoc, Menelae) nefandas,
primaque lux nostri tecum fuit illa pericli.
longa referre mora est quae consilioque manuque
utiliter feci spatiosi tempore belli:
post acies primas, urbis se moenibus hostes
continuere diu, nec aperti **copia Martis**
ulla fuit; decimo pugnavimus anno.
quid facis interea, qui nil nisi proelia nosti?
quis tuus usus erat? nam si mea facta requiris,
hostibus insidior, fossas munimine cingo,
consolor socios ut longi **taedia** belli
mente ferant placida, doceo quo simus alendi
armandique modo, mittor quo postulat usus.

Ovid, Metamorphoses XIII.200

Words
copia 1f (here) = opportunity; **taedia** 2npl = boredom.
Names
Priamus 2m = Priam, king of Troy; **Antenor** (acc **Antenora**) = Antenor, one of Priam's counsellors; **Mars Martis** 3m = Mars, god of war: war.

110. Callisto, with whom Jupiter has had an affair, is punished by Juno by being turned into a bear.

"You won't get away with this!" Juno said. "I'll take away that beauty that my husband delighted in so much." And she got hold of Callisto by the hair and forced her down on all fours.

bracchia coeperunt nigris horrescere **villis**
curvarique manus et **aduncos** crescere in **ungues**.
neve preces animos et verba precantia **flectant**,
posse loqui eripitur: vox iracunda minaxque
plenaque terroris rauco de gutture fertur.
mens antiqua manet (facta quoque mansit in **ursa**),
assiduoque manus ad caelum et sidera tollit
ingratumque Iovem, nequeat cum dicere, sentit.
a, quotiens sola non ausa quiescere silva
ante domum quondamque suis erravit in agris!
a, quotiens per saxa canum **latratibus** acta est,
venatrixque metu venantum territa fugit!
saepe feris latuit visis, oblita quid esset,
ursaque conspectos in montibus horruit **ursos**,
pertimuitque lupos, quamvis **pater** esset in illis.

Ovid, Metamorphoses II.478

Words

villi 2mpl = hair; **aduncus** adj = hooked; **unguis unguis** 3m = claw; **flecto** 3 (here) = influence; **ursa** 1f/**ursus** 2m = bear; **assiduo** adv = repeatedly; **latratus** 4m = barking; **venatrix venatricis** 3f = huntress (which Callisto had been); **pater** = Callisto's father Lycaon, who had been turned into a wolf.

111. Eudemus' dream comes true, but not wholly as he had expected.

Xenophon also, in his account of the expedition he went on with Cyrus, records some dreams which turned out true. Nor is he the only philosopher to accept such things:

Aristoteles scribit Eudemum **Cyprium**, familiarem suum, iter in Macedoniam facientem **Pheras** venisse, quae erat urbs in Thessalia tum admodum nobilis, ab Alexandro autem tyranno crudeli dominatu tenebatur; in eo igitur oppido ita graviter aegrum Eudemum fuisse ut omnes medici diffiderent; ei visum in quiete egregia facie iuvenem dicere fore ut perbrevi convalesceret, paucisque diebus interiturum Alexandrum tyrannum, ipsum autem Eudemum **quinquennio post** domum esse rediturum. atque ita quidem prima statim scribit Aristoteles consecuta, et convaluisse Eudemum, et ab uxoris fratribus interfectum tyrannum. quinto autem anno exeunte, cum esset spes ex illo somnio in Cyprum ex Sicilia esse rediturum, proeliantem eum ad **Syracusas** occidisse; ex quo ita illud somnium esse interpretatum ut, cum animus Eudemi e corpore excesserit, tum domum revertisse videatur.

Cicero, On Divination I.52

Words
quinquennio post = within the next five years
Names
Cyprius adj = of Cyprus; **Pherae** 1fpl = Pherae; **Syracusae** 1fpl = Syracuse, in Sicily.

111

112. An attempt by an innkeeper to put the blame for a murder on an innocent man.

Two businessmen, one of whom was carrying a large amount of cash, met while travelling, and became friendly. They went to an inn together, and had dinner.

cenati discubuerunt ibidem. caupo autem (nam ita dicitur post inventum, cum in alio maleficio deprehensus est) cum illum alterum, videlicet qui nummos haberet, **animum advertisset**, noctu postquam illos **artius** iam, ut ex lassitudine, dormire sensit, accessit et alterius eorum, qui sine nummis erat, gladium e vagina eduxit et illum alterum occidit, nummos abstulit, gladium cruentum in vaginam recondit, ipse se in suum lectum recepit. ille autem, cuius gladio occisio erat facta, multo ante lucem surrexit, comitem illum suum inclamavit semel et saepius. illum somno impeditum non respondere existimavit; ipse gladium et cetera quae secum attulerat sustulit, solus profectus est. caupo non multo post conclamat hominem esse occisum et cum quibusdam **diversoribus** illum qui ante exierat consequitur in via. hominem comprehendit, gladium eius e vagina educit, repperit cruentum. homo in urbem ab illis deducitur ac reus fit.

Cicero, On Invention II.14

Words

animum advertisset = **animadvertisset**; **artius** = rather soundly; **diversor diversoris** 3m = guest.

113. Servius Sulpicius writes to Cicero to tell him about the murder of their mutual friend Marcellus.

When I got to Athens I met Marcus Marcellus, and spent the day with him. I was going to go on to Boeotia, and he said he was shortly going to sail back to Italy.

post diem tertium eius diei, cum ab Athenis proficisci in animo haberem, circiter hora decima noctis P. Postumius, familiaris eius, ad me venit et mihi nuntiavit Marcellum post cenae tempus a P. Magio Cilione, familiare eius, **pugione** percussum esse et duo vulnera accepisse, unum in stomacho, alterum in capite **secundum** aurem; sperare tamen eum vivere posse; Magium se ipsum interfecisse postea; se a Marcello ad me missum esse qui haec nuntiaret et rogaret uti medicos ei mitterem. itaque medicos coegi et **e vestigio eo** sum profectus prima luce. cum non longe a **Piraeo** abessem, **puer Acidini** obviam mihi venit cum **codicillis** in quibus erat scriptum paulo ante lucem Marcellum diem suum obisse. ita vir clarissimus ab homine deterrimo acerbissima morte est affectus et, cui inimici propter dignitatem pepercerant, inventus est amicus qui ei mortem offerret.

Sulpicius, in Cicero, Letters to Friends IV.12

Words

pugio pugionis 3m = dagger; **secundum** (+acc) = behind; **e vestigio eo** = straightaway; **puer** (here) = slave; **codicilli** 2mpl = a letter.

Names

Piraeus 2m = the Piraeus, the harbour of Athens; **Acidinus** 2m = Acidinus, a friend of Sulpicius and Marcellus.

114. Lysander is surprised and impressed by Cyrus's expertise as a gardener.

So that you may know that no activity is as appropriate for a prince as gardening, listen to what Socrates says about Cyrus the Persian prince, a man of great power and intellect:

cum Lysander **Lacedaemonius**, vir summae virtutis, venisset ad eum **Sardes** eique dona a sociis attulisset, Cyrum et ceteris in rebus **communem** erga Lysandrum atque humanum fuisse, et ei quendam **consaeptum** agrum diligenter **consitum** ostendisse. cum autem admiraretur Lysander et **proceritates** arborum et directos in **quincuncem** ordines et humum **subactam** atque puram et suavitatem odorum qui afflarentur ex floribus, tum eum dixisse mirari se non modo diligentiam sed etiam sollertiam eius a quo essent illa dimensa atque discripta; et Cyrum respondisse "**atqui** ego ista sum omnia dimensus, mei sunt ordines, mea discriptio; multae etiam istarum arborum mea manu sunt satae." tum Lysandrum, intuentem **purpuram** eius et **nitorem** corporis **ornatum**que Persicum multo auro multisque gemmis, dixisse "recte vero te, Cyre, beatum **ferunt**, quoniam virtuti tuae fortuna coniuncta est!"

Cicero, On Old Age 59

Words

communis adj = hospitable; **consaeptus** adj = fenced in; **consitus** adj = laid out; **proceritas proceritatis** 3f = height; **quincunx quincuncis** 3m = a quincunx, a method of planting trees in groups of five; **subactus** adj = carefully dug; **atqui** = actually; **purpura** 1f = purple cloak; **nitor nitoris** 3m = healthy appearance; **ornatus** 4m = dress; **ferunt** (here) = they call.

Names

Lacedaemonius adj = Spartan; **Sardes Sardium** 3fpl = Sardis, in Asia Minor.

115. Two more stories showing that dreams come true, though not always as expected.

Let us leave our discussion of the truthfulness of oracles, and move on to dreams.

apud **Agathoclem** scriptum in historia est **Hamilcarem Carthaginiensem**, cum oppugnaret **Syracusas**, visum esse audire vocem se postridie cenaturum **Syracusis**. cum autem is dies inluxisset, magnam seditionem in castris eius inter **Poenos** et **Siculos** milites esse factam; quod cum sensissent **Syracusani**, improviso eos in castra inrupisse, **Hamilcarem**que ab iis vivum esse sublatum. ita res somnium comprobavit. plena exemplorum est historia: P. Decius vero, cum esset tribunus militum, a **Samnitibus**que premeretur noster exercitus, cum pericula proeliorum iniret audacius moneretur que ut cautior esset, dixit se sibi in somnis visum esse, cum in mediis hostibus versaretur, occidere cum maxima gloria. et tum quidem incolumis obsidione liberavit; **post triennium** autem, cum consul esset, **devovit se** et in aciem **Latinorum** inrupit armatus. quo eius facto superati sunt et deleti **Latini**. cuius mors ita gloriosa fuit ut eandem concupisceret filius.

Cicero, On Divination I.50

Words

apud (+acc) (here) = in the writings of; **post triennium** = after three years; **devovit se** = [he] dedicated himself (to the gods).

Names

Agathocles Agathoclis 3m = Agathocles, a historian; **Hamilcar Hamilcaris** 3m = Hamilcar, a Carthaginian (**Carthaginiensis** 3m); **Syracusae** 1fpl = Syracuse, in Sicily; **Poenus** adj = Carthaginian; **Siculus** adj = Sicilian; **Syracusani** 2mpl = Syracusans; **Samnites Samnitium** 3mpl = Samnites; **Latini** 2mpl = Latins.

115

116. Cicero explains why, in the Civil War against Caesar, he left Pompey's forces.

My decision to join Pompey was more a matter of thinking of my reputation than of good sense; and I changed my mind not so much because of the danger as because of the problems I found in Pompey's camp:

primum neque magnas copias neque bellicosas; deinde, **extra** ducem paucosque praeterea (de principibus loquor), reliqui in ipso bello rapaces, deinde in oratione ita crudeles ut ipsam victoriam horrerem. quid quaeris? nihil boni praeter causam. quae cum vidissem, desperans victoriam primum coepi suadere pacem, cuius fueram semper auctor, deinde, cum **ab** ea sententia Pompeius valde **abhorreret**, suadere institui ut bellum duceret. hoc interdum probabat et in ea sententia videbatur fore, et fuisset fortasse, nisi quadam ex pugna coepisset suis militibus confidere. ex eo tempore vir ille summus nullus imperator fuit. **signa tirone** exercitu **cum** legionibus robustissimis **contulit**; victus turpissime amissis etiam castris solus fugit. hunc ego mihi belli finem feci nec putavi, cum integri pares non fuissemus, fractos superiores fore: discessi ab eo bello, in quo aut in acie cadendum fuit aut in aliquas insidias incidendum aut deveniendum in victoris manus aut capiendus tamquam exsilio locus aut **consciscenda** mors voluntaria.

Cicero, Letters to Friends VII.3

Words

extra (+acc) (here) = apart from; **abhorreo** 2 **ab** = shrink from; **signa confero** (etc) **cum** (+abl) = join battle with; **tiro tironis** adj = inexperienced, novice; **conscisco** 3 = bring upon oneself.

116

117. A murderer is brought to justice because of a dream.

And who would contest the truth of those dreams that the Stoics are always citing? One of which is as follows:

cum duo quidam **Arcades** familiares iter una facerent et **Megaram** venissent, alterum **ad** cauponem **devertisse**, ad hospitem alterum. qui ut cenati quiescerent, nocte visum esse in somnis ei qui erat in hospitio illum alterum orare ut subveniret, quod sibi a caupone interitus pararetur; eum primo perterritum somnio surrexisse; dein, cum se collegisset idque visum **pro nihilo habendum** esse **duxisset**, recubuisse; tum ei dormienti eundem illum visum esse rogare ut, quoniam sibi vivo non subvenisset, mortem suam ne inultam esse pateretur; se, interfectum, in plaustrum a caupone esse coniectum et supra **stercus** iniectum; petere ut mane ad portam adesset priusquam plaustrum ex oppido exiret. hoc vero eum somnio commotum mane **bubulco praesto** ad portam **fuisse**, quaesisse ex eo quid esset in plaustro; illum perterritum fugisse, mortuum erutum esse, cauponem re patefacta poenas dedisse.

Cicero, On Divination I.56

Words

deverto 3 **deverti ad** = go to stay with; **pro nihilo habere** = disregard, pay little attention to; **duco** (here) **duxi** = think; **stercus stercoris** 3n = manure; **bubulcus** 2m = a ploughman, farmer; **praesto sum** (+dat) = approach.

Names

Arcas Arcadis 3m = Arcadian; **Megara** 1f = Megara, in Greece.

118. Gyges immorally rises to power when he finds a magic ring.

If we have made any kind of progress in philosophy at all, we must acknowledge that, even if we are unobserved by gods and men, we must never act avariciously or unjustly.

hinc ille Gyges **inducitur** a **Platone**, qui, cum terra **discessisset** magnis quibusdam imbribus, descendit in illum **hiatum** aeneumque equum, ut ferunt fabulae, animadvertit, cuius in lateribus fores essent; quibus apertis, corpus hominis mortui vidit magnitudine inusitata anulumque aureum in digito; quem ut detraxit, ipse induit, (erat autem regius pastor) tum in concilium se pastorum recepit. ibi cum **palam** eius anuli ad palmam converterat, a nullo videbatur, ipse autem omnia videbat; idem rursus videbatur, cum in locum anulum inverterat. itaque, hac opportunitate anuli usus, reginae **stuprum intulit** eaque **adiutrice** regem dominum interemit, sustulit quos obstare arbitrabatur, nec in his eum facinoribus quisquam potuit videre. sic repente anuli beneficio rex exortus est **Lydiae**. hunc igitur ipsum anulum si habeat sapiens, nihilo plus sibi licere putet peccare quam si non haberet: honesta enim bonis viris, non occulta quaeruntur.

Cicero, On Duties III.38

Words
hinc = "to illustrate this point"; **induco** 3 = mention; **discedo** 3 **discessi** (here) = split open; **hiatus** 4m = gap; **pala** 1f = the bezel of a ring (the part where the stone would be); **stuprum infero** (etc) (+dat) = seduce; **adiutrix adiutricis** 3f = helper.

Names
Plato Platonis 3m = Plato, the philosopher; **Lydia** 1f = Lydia, in Asia Minor.

119. Cicero writes to Atticus about the rude behaviour of Atticus' sister Pomponia, who is the wife of Cicero's brother Quintus.

Next morning we left Arpinum. Because of the holiday Quintus was going to stay at his farm at Arcae and we went there for lunch.

quo ut venimus, humanissime Quintus "Pomponia," inquit, "tu **invita mulieres**, ego vero **adscivero pueros**." nihil potuit, mihi quidem ut visum est, dulcius, idque cum verbis tum animo ac vultu. at illa, audientibus nobis, "ego ipsa sum," inquit, "hic **hospita**"; id autem ex eo, ut opinor, quod antecesserat **Statius** ut prandium nobis videret. tum Quintus "en!" inquit mihi, "haec ego patior cotidie." dices "**quid, quaeso, istuc erat**?" magnum: itaque me ipsum commoverat; sic absurde et aspere verbis vultuque responderat. dissimulavi dolens. discubuimus omnes praeter illam, cui tamen Quintus **de mensa** misit; illa reiecit. quid multa? nihil meo fratre lenius, nihil asperius tua sorore mihi visum est; et multa praetereo quae tum mihi maiori stomacho quam ipsi Quinto fuerunt. ego inde **Aquinum**. Quintus in **Arcano** remansit et **Aquinum** ad me postridie mane venit mihique narravit nec secum illam dormire voluisse et cum discessura esset fuisse eius modi qualem ego vidissem. haec ad te scripsi, fortasse pluribus quam necesse fuit, ut videres tuas quoque esse **partes** instituendi et monendi.

Cicero, Letters to Atticus V.1

Words

invita: i.e call them in for lunch; **mulieres** (here) = the female slaves; **adscio** 4 = call; **puer** (here) = (male) slave; **hospita** 1f = guest; **quid istuc erat** = "what was the significance of that?"; **de mensa** = "some food from the table"; **partes** 3fpl (here) = responsibility.

Names

Statius 2m = Statius, Quintus's steward, who will have gone on ahead to open up the house; **Aquinum** 2n = Aquinum, where Cicero had a house; **Arcanum** 2n = the farm at Arcae.

120. Simonides gets an unexpected reward for a poem he has written about the ungrateful Scopas, and at the same time discovers the most important principle of memory.

I am not like Themistocles, who is supposed to have preferred forgetfulness to remembering: rather I give thanks to Simonides, who is said to have been the first to give attention to the art of memory.

dicunt enim, cum cenaret Simonides apud **Scopam**, fortunatum hominem et nobilem, cecinissetque id carmen quod in eum scripsisset, in quo multa, ornandi causa more poetarum, in **Castorem** scripta et **Pollucem** fuissent, nimis illum sordide Simonidi dixisse se dimidium eius ei quod **pactus esset** pro illo carmine daturum; reliquum a suis **Tyndaridis**, quos aeque laudasset, peteret, si ei videretur. paulo post esse ferunt nuntiatum Simonidi ut **prodiret**: iuvenes stare ad ianuam duo quosdam, qui eum magno opere evocaret; surrexisse illum, **prodisse**, vidisse neminem; hoc interim spatio conclave illud, ubi epularetur **Scopas**, concidisse; ea ruina, ipsum cum cognatis oppressum suis interisse. quos cum **humare** vellent sui, neque possent **obtritos internoscere** ullo modo, Simonides dicitur ex eo, quod meminisset quo eorum loco quisque cubuisset, demonstrator **uniuscuiusque** sepeliendi fuisse; hac tum re admonitus invenisse fertur ordinem esse maxime qui memoriae lumen adferret.

Cicero, On the Orator II.351

Words

paciscor 3dep pactus sum = agree, promise; **prodeo prodire** = come out; **humo** 1 = bury; **obtritos** = "the crushed bodies"; **internosco** 3 = distinguish between; **unusquisque** = every single one.

Names

Scopas Scopae 1m = Scopas; **Castor Castoris** 3m and **Pollux Pollucis** 3m, the two gods, were the sons of Tyndareus (**Tyndaridae** mpl).

121. **Jupiter foretells the future of Ascanius [Iulus], the son of Aeneas, and his descendants, from whom the Roman people shall arise.**

"Aeneas shall wage a great war in Italy, and shall subdue its fierce tribes, and he shall build his city there: after three years he shall be king in Latium.

at puer Ascanius, cui nunc cognomen Iulo
additur (**Ilus** erat, dum res stetit **Ilia** regno),
triginta magnos volvendis mensibus orbes
imperio explebit, regnumque ab sede **Latini**
transferet, et **Longam** multa vi muniet **Albam**.
hic iam ter centum totos regnabitur annos
gente sub **Hectorea**, donec regina sacerdos
Marte gravis geminam partu dabit **Ilia** prolem.
inde, lupae fulvo nutricis **tegmine** laetus,
Romulus excipiet gentem et **Mavortia** condet
moenia, Romanosque suo de nomine dicet.
his ego nec **metas** rerum nec tempora pono:
imperium sine fine dedi."

Virgil, Aeneid I.267

Words

triginta...orbes: i.e. thirty years; **gravis** (here) = pregnant; **tegmen tegminis** 3n = protection; **meta** 1f = boundary.

Names

Ilus 2m: another name of Ascanius; **Ilius** adj (line 2) = Trojan; **Latinus** 2m = Latinus, king of Latium; **Alba Longa** 1f = Alba Longa; **Hectoreus** adj = of Hector; **Mars Martis** 3m = Mars, god of war; **Ilia** 1f (line 8) = Ilia, mother of Romulus and Remus; **Mavortius** adj = of Mars, warlike.

122. Aeneas describes how he and the Trojans set sail before dawn and, as the sun rose, saw the coast of Italy for the first time.

While it was still not yet light, the helmsman Palinurus got up and gauged the winds and took note of the movements of the constellations in the silent heavens.

postquam cuncta videt caelo **constare** sereno,
dat clarum e puppi signum; nos castra movemus
temptamusque viam et velorum pandimus alas.
iamque **rubescebat** stellis **Aurora** fugatis,
cum procul obscuros colles humilemque videmus
Italiam. Italiam primus conclamat **Achates**;
Italiam laeto socii clamore salutant.
tum pater **Anchises** magnum **cratera** corona
induit implevitque mero, divosque vocavit,
stans celsa in puppi:
"di maris et terrae tempestatumque potentes,
ferte viam vento facilem et **spirate** secundi."
crebrescunt optatae aurae portusque **patescit**
iam propior, templumque apparet in arce **Minervae**;
vela **legunt** socii et proras ad litora torquent.

Virgil, Aeneid III.518

Words

consto 1 = to be all right; **rubesco** 3 = become red; **crater crateris** (acc **cratera**) 3m = bowl; **induo** 3 **indui** (here) = surround, wreathe; **spiro** 1 = blow; **crebresco** 3 = grow stronger; **patesco** 3 = open up; **lego** 3 (here) = furl.

Names

Aurora 1f = the dawn; **Achates Achatis** 3m = Achates, a Trojan; **Anchises Anchisis** 3m = Anchises, Aeneas's father; **Minerva** 1f = the goddess Minerva.

123. Aeneas and some of his men, sailing up the River Tiber in their ship, encounter Pallas, the son of King Evander, whom they are seeking.

When the bold Pallas saw the ship approaching, he told his men to continue the sacrifice. He himself seized his spear and went up on to a small hill:

> "iuvenes, quae causa **subegit**
> ignotas temptare vias? quo tenditis?" inquit,
> "qui genus? unde domo? pacemne huc fertis an arma?"
> tum pater Aeneas puppi sic fatur ab alta,
> paciferaeque manu ramum praetendit olivae:
> "**Troiugenas** ac tela vides inimica **Latinis**,
> quos illi bello profugos egere superbo.
> Evandrum petimus. ferte haec et dicite lectos
> **Dardaniae** venisse duces socia arma rogantes."
> obstipuit tanto percussus nomine Pallas:
> "egredere, o quicumque es," ait, "coramque parentem
> adloquere ac nostris succede penatibus hospes."
> excepitque manu dextramque amplexus inhaesit;
> progressi subeunt luco fluviumque relinquunt.
> *Virgil, Aeneid VIII.112*

Words
subigo 3 subegi = drive, impel.
Names
Troiugenae 1mpl = Trojans; **Latini** 2mpl = Latins; **Dardania** 1f = Troy.

124. While bringing his wife Eurydice up from the Underworld, Orpheus disobeys his instructions and looks back at her.

When Orpheus sang in the Underworld, the ghosts and the insubstantial lightless shades were moved...the three mouths of Cerberus ceased their barking, and Ixion's wheel stopped in its course.

iamque pedem referens casus evaserat omnes,
redditaque **Eurydice** superas veniebat ad auras,
pone sequens (namque hanc dederat **Proserpina** legem),
cum subita incautum dementia cepit amantem,
ignoscenda quidem, scirent si ignoscere Manes:
restitit, **Eurydicen**que suam iam luce sub ipsa,
immemor (heu!) victusque animi respexit. ibi omnis
effusus labor atque immitis rupta tyranni
foedera, terque fragor **stagnis** auditus **Avernis**.
illa, "quis et me", inquit, "miseram et te perdidit, Orpheu,
quis tantus furor? en, iterum crudelia retro
fata vocant, conditque natantia lumina somnus.
iamque vale: feror ingenti circumdata nocte
invalidasque tibi tendens, heu non tua, palmas."

Virgil, Georgic IV.485

Words
pone adv = behind; **stagnum** 2n = marsh, swamp.
Names
Eurydice (acc **Eurydicen**) f = Eurydice; **Proserpina** 1f = Proserpina, goddess of the Underworld; **Avernus** adj = of Avernus, in the Underworld.

124

125. Aeneas in the Underworld meets the ghost of Dido, who has killed herself for love of him.

Not far from here are the Fields of Mourning: here in a dark forest dwell the shades of those who have died for love. Amongst those who wandered in that great wood was Dido, who had so recently taken her own life:

           quam Troius heros
ut primum iuxta stetit agnovitque per umbras,
demisit lacrimas dulcique adfatus amore est:
"infelix Dido, verus mihi nuntius ergo
venerat exstinctam ferroque extrema secutam?
funeris (heu!) tibi causa fui? per sidera iuro,
per superos et si qua fides tellure sub ima est,
invitus, regina, tuo de litore cessi.
sed me iussa deum, quae nunc has ire per umbras,
per loca **senta situ**, cogunt, noctemque profundam,
imperiis egere suis; nec credere quivi
hunc tantum tibi me discessu ferre dolorem.
siste gradum teque aspectu ne subtrahe nostro:
quem fugis? extremum fato quod te adloquor hoc est."

                     Virgil, Aeneid VI.451

Words
senta situ = dismal with neglect.

126. Turnus has been waiting in ambush for Aeneas. When he is told of the defeat of his main army, he sets out to relieve it, and suddenly encounters Aeneas, but nightfall prevents them from fighting.

Meanwhile Acca brought news of the disaster to Turnus in his ambush: the Volscians had been destroyed, Camilla killed; the enemy were carrying all before them, and the panic had almost reached the city.

ille furens (et saeva Iovis sic numina poscunt)
deserit obsessos colles, nemora aspera linquit.
vix e conspectu exierat campumque tenebat,
cum pater Aeneas saltus ingressus apertos
exsuperatque iugum silvaque evadit opaca.
sic ambo ad muros rapidi totoque feruntur
agmine, nec longis inter se passibus absunt;
ac simul Aeneas fumantes pulvere campos
prospexit longe **Laurentia**que agmina vidit,
et saevum **Aenean** agnovit Turnus in armis,
adventumque pedum **flatus**que audivit equorum.
continuoque ineant pugnas et proelia temptent,
ni roseus fessos iam gurgite **Phoebus Hibero**
tingat equos, noctemque die labente reducat.
considunt castris ante urbem et moenia vallant.

Virgil, Aeneid XI.901

Words

flatus 4m = breath, breathing.

Names

Laurens Laurentis adj = Laurentine; **Aenean** is acc of Aeneas; **Phoebus** 2m = Apollo (here in his capacity as Sun-god); **Hiberus** adj = Spanish: western.

127. Polydorus, the youngest son of King Priam of Troy, had been sent away by his father when the war against the Greeks began to turn against them, but was treacherously killed by his guardian, the king of Thrace. Aeneas relates how he found the body of Polydorus and gave him a proper burial.

While I tried to pull the shoot from the earth, a terrible omen occurred: blood dripped from the severed roots...a mournful voice arose from the earth: "Why do you torture me, Aeneas? Leave me, and leave this place: for I am Polydorus."

hunc Polydorum auri quondam cum pondere magno
infelix Priamus furtim mandarat alendum
Threicio regi, cum iam diffideret armis
Dardaniae, cingique urbem obsidione videret.
ille, ut opes fractae **Teucrum** et Fortuna recessit,
fas omne abrumpit: Polydorum **obtruncat**, et auro
vi potitur. quid non mortalia pectora cogis,
auri sacra fames! postquam pavor ossa reliquit
delectos populi ad proceres primumque parentem
monstra deum refero, et quae sit sententia posco.
omnibus idem animus: scelerata excedere terra.
ergo **instauramus** Polydoro funus, et ingens
aggreditur tumulo tellus, animamque sepulcro
condimus et magna **supremum** voce **ciemus**.
                    Virgil, Aeneid III.49

Words

obtrunco 1 = murder; **monstra...refero** = "I explain[-ed] about this apparition from the gods"; **instauro** 1 = hold; **supremum ciemus** = "we call[-ed] upon him for the last time".

Names

Threicius rex = Polymestor, king of Thrace; **Dardania** 1f = Troy; **Teucri Teucrum** 2mpl = Trojans.

128. Venus seduces her husband Vulcan to get him to make some armour for her son Aeneas.

Venus was terrified by the threats of the Laurentines against Aeneas. She went to Vulcan in their gilded bedroom, and spoke to him, breathing divine love into her words:

"dum bello **Argolici** vastabant **Pergama** reges,
non ullum auxilium miseris, non arma rogavi
artis opisque tuae, nec te, carissime coniunx,
incassumve tuos volui exercere labores,
quamvis et **Priami** deberem plurima natis,
et durum Aeneae flevissem saepe laborem.
nunc, Iovis imperiis, **Rutulorum** constitit oris:
ergo eadem supplex venio et sanctum mihi numen
arma rogo, genetrix nato. te **filia Nerei**,
te potuit lacrimis **Tithonia** flectere **coniunx**."
dixerat et niveis hinc atque hinc diva lacertis
cunctantem amplexu molli fovet. ille repente
accepit solitam flammam, notusque **medullas**
intravit calor et labefacta per ossa cucurrit;
sensit laeta dolis et formae conscia coniunx.

Virgil, Aeneid VIII.374

Words

incassum adv = in vain; **medulla** 1f = heart.

Names

Argolicus adj = Greek; **Pergama** 2npl = Pergama, the stronghold of Troy; **Priamus** 2m = Priam, king of Troy; **Rutuli** 2mpl = Rutulians, an Italian tribe; **filia Nerei**, the sea-goddess Thetis, and **Tithonia coniunx**, Aurora, goddess of the dawn and wife of Tithonus, both had armour made for their sons, Achilles and Memnon respectively, by Vulcan.

129. Juno recruits the monster Allecto to break up the new alliance between the Trojans and the Latins.

So Juno furiously descended to the Earth. She summoned from the abode of the Furies in the infernal darkness Allecto, who delights in nothing more than grim war and strife and anger.

odit et ipse pater **Pluton**, odere sorores
Tartareae monstrum: tot sese vertit in ora,
tam saevae facies, tot **pullulat** atra colubris.
quam Iuno his **acuit** verbis et talia fatur:
"hunc mihi da proprium, virgo **sata Nocte**, laborem,
hanc operam, ne noster honos infractave cedat
fama loco, neu conubiis **ambire Latinum**
Aeneadae possint Italosve obsidere fines.
tu potes **unanimos** armare in proelia fratres
atque odiis versare domos, tibi nomina mille,
mille nocendi artes. fecundum **concute** pectus,
dissice compositam pacem, sere crimina belli;
arma velit poscatque simul rapiatque iuventus!"
Virgil, Aeneid VII.327

Words
pullulo 1 = throb, seethe; **acuo** 3 = urge on; **ambio** 4 = cajole, get round; **unanimus** adj = of one mind, harmonious; **concutio** 3 (here) = arouse; **dissicio** 3 = break up.
Names
Pluton Plutonis 3m = Pluto, god of the Underworld; **Tartareus** adj = of Tartarus, in the Underworld; **sata Nocte** = daughter of Night; **Latinus** 2m = Latinus, king of Latium; **Aeneadae** mpl = the people of Aeneas.

130. The end of the single combat between Aeneas and Turnus: as he summons up his resources for a final onslaught, Turnus' strength gives out.

The nymph Juturna saw that there was nothing more she could do for her brother Turnus, now that Jupiter himself had intervened. She veiled her head, groaned piteously, and plunged down into the depths of her river.

Aeneas instat contra telumque coruscat
ingens, arboreum, et saevo sic pectore fatur:
"quae nunc deinde mora est? aut quid iam, Turne, retractas?
non cursu, saevis certandum est comminus armis."
ille, caput **quassans**, "non me tua fervida terrent
dicta, ferox: di me terrent, et Iuppiter hostis."
nec plura effatus saxum circumspicit ingens,
saxum antiquum, ingens, campo quod forte iacebat,
limes agro positus **litem ut discerneret** arvis.
ille manu raptum trepida torquebat in hostem,
sed neque currentem se nec cognoscit euntem,
tollentemve manu saxumve immane moventem;
genua labant, gelidus concrevit frigore sanguis.
tum lapis ipse viri vacuum per inane volutus
nec spatium evasit totum neque pertulit ictum.
                    Virgil, Aeneid XII.887

Words

quasso 1 = shake; **litem ut discerneret** = "to resolve any disagreement".

131. An Epicurean philosopher shows by his actions that Epicureans do not only act in their own interests: demonstrating that natural feelings are stronger than doctrinaire philosophy.

If an evil-doer were supremely powerful, like Crassus or Pompey (though of course they are both men of upright character who would not act like this), he could easily do what he wanted with impunity.

quam multa vero iniuste fieri possunt quae nemo possit reprehendere! si te amicus tuus moriens rogaverit ut **hereditatem** reddas suae filiae, nec usquam id scripserit nec cuiquam dixerit, quid facies? tu quidem reddes; ipse Epicurus fortasse redderet; ut Sextus Peducaeus, cum doctus, tum omnium vir optimus et iustissimus, cum sciret nemo eum rogatum a C. Plotio, equite Romano splendido **Nursino**, ultro ad mulierem venit eique nihil **opinanti** viri mandatum exposuit **hereditatem**que reddidit. sed ego ex te quaero, quoniam idem tu certe fecisses, nonne intellegas eo maiorem vim esse naturae quod ipsi vos, qui omnia ad vestrum **commodum** et, ut ipsi dicitis, ad voluptatem referatis, tamen ea faciatis e quibus appareat non voluptatem vos sed officium sequi, plusque rectam naturam quam rationem pravam valere?

Cicero, On the Boundaries of Good and Evil II.57

Words
hereditas hereditatis 3f = legacy; **opinor** 1dep (here) = expect; **commodum** 2n (here) = interest, advantage.
Names
Nursinus adj = of Nursia.

131

132. Cyrus, on his deathbed, affirms his belief that the soul is immortal.

According to Xenophon, Cyrus, as he lay dying, said as follows: "Do not believe, my sons, that when I leave you, I shall no longer exist: while I have lived, you have not been able to see my soul, but you have known that it was there from what I have done. So you may believe that it still exists, though my body does not.

mihi quidem numquam persuaderi potuit animos dum in corporibus essent mortalibus vivere, cum excessissent ex eis emori; nec vero tum animum esse **insipientem** cum ex **insipienti** corpore evasisset, sed cum, omni admixtione corporis liberatus, purus et integer esse coepisset, tum esse sapientem. atque etiam, cum hominis natura morte dissolvitur, ceterarum rerum perspicuum est quo quaeque discedat, abeunt enim illuc omnia unde orta sunt; animus autem solus nec cum adest nec cum discessit apparet. iam vero videtis nihil esse morti tam simile quam somnum; atqui dormientium animi maxime declarant divinitatem suam; multa enim, cum **remissi** et liberi sunt, futura prospiciunt; ex quo intellegitur quales futuri sint cum se plane ex corporis vinclis relaxaverint. qua re, si haec ita sunt, sic me **colitote**," inquit, "ut deum, sin una est interiturus animus cum corpore, vos tamen, deos verentes, qui hanc omnem pulchritudinem tuentur et regunt, memoriam nostri pie inviolateque servabitis."

Cicero, On Old Age 79

Words

insipiens insipientis adj = foolish, unwise; **remissus** adj = relaxed; **colitote** is pl imperative of colo, = **colite**.

133. Man cannot live properly without human companionship, even if he has all the other necessities for life.

The experience of all kinds of men shows that without friendship life is no life at all: or at least, no kind of life for a free man.

quin etiam si quis asperitate ea est et immanitate naturae, congressus ut hominum fugiat atque oderit, qualem fuisse **Athenis Timonem** nescioquem **accepimus**, tamen is pati non possit ut non **anquirat** aliquem apud quem **evomat virus** acerbitatis suae. atque hoc maxime iudicaretur, si quid tale posset contingere, ut aliquis nos deus ex hac hominum frequentia tolleret et in solitudine **uspiam** collocaret atque ibi suppeditans omnium rerum quas natura desiderat abundantiam et copiam, hominis omnino aspiciendi potestatem eriperet: quis tam esset ferreus qui eam vitam ferre posset, cuique non auferret fructum voluptatum omnium solitudo? verum ergo illud est, quod a **Tarentino Archyta**, ut opinor, dici solitum nostros senes commemorare audivi ab aliis senibus auditum: **si quis in caelum ascendisset** naturamque mundi et pulchritudinem siderum perspexisset, insuavem illam admirationem ei fore, quae iucundissima fuisset si aliquem cui narraret habuisset.

Cicero, On Friendship 87

Words

accipio (here) = hear; **anquiro** 3 = seek out; **evomo** 3 = spit out; **virus** 2n = venom; **uspiam** adv = somewhere; **si...ascendisset**: i.e. if the person were to do this alone, without companionship.

Names

Timon Timonis 3m = Timon, a proverbially misanthropic man from Athens (**Athenae** 1fpl); **Tarentinus** adj = of Tarentum (Taranto); **Archytas** 1m = Archytas, a philosopher.

134. Unlike Hercules, who saw clearly the two possible paths through life, most of us make up our minds as to what we are going to be in a haphazard way.

But above all, we must decide what sort of people we want to be, and what career we ought to pursue: which is the most difficult decision of all.

ineunte enim adulescentia, cum est maxima **imbecillitas** consilii, tum id sibi quisque genus aetatis **degendae** constituit, quod maxime adamavit. itaque ante implicatur aliquo certo genere cursuque vivendi quam potuit quod optimum est iudicare. nam quod Herculem Prodicus dicit, ut est apud Xenophontem, cum primum pubesceret (quod tempus a natura ad deligendum quam quisque viam vivendi sit ingressurus datum est), exisse in solitudinem atque ibi sedentem diu secum dubitasse (cum duas cerneret vias, unam voluptatis, alteram virtutis) utram ingredi melius esset; hoc Herculi potuit fortasse contingere, nobis non item, qui imitamur quos cuique visum est, atque ad eorum studia institutaque impellimur; plerumque autem, parentium praeceptis imbuti, ad eorum consuetudinem moremque deducimur; alii multitudinis iudicio feruntur, quaeque maiori parti pulcherrima videntur, ea maxime exoptant; nonnulli tamen, sive felicitate quadam sive bonitate naturae, sine parentium disciplina rectam vitae secuti sunt viam.

Cicero, On Duties I.117

Words
imbecillitas imbecillitatis 3f = weakness; **dego** 3 = lead (one's life).

135. Sometimes it is right not to keep a promise.

To take an example from mythology, the Sun-god promised his son anything he wanted: he wanted to drive the chariot of the sun. He drove it, got out of control, and had to be destroyed by Jupiter's thunderbolt. How much better if that promise had not been kept!

quid, quod Theseus **exegit** promissum a Neptuno? cui cum tres optationes Neptunus dedisset, optavit interitum **Hippolyti** filii, cum is patri suspectus esset **de noverca**; quo optato impetrato Theseus in maximis fuit luctibus. quid, quod Agamemnon, cum devovisset Dianae quod in suo regno pulcherrimum natum esset illo anno, immolavit **Iphigeniam**, quia nihil erat eo quidem anno natum pulchrius? promissum potius non faciendum quam tam taetrum facinus admittendum fuit. ergo et promissa non facienda nonnumquam, neque semper deposita reddenda. si gladium quis apud te sana mente deposuerit, repetat insaniens, reddere peccatum sit, officium non reddere. quid? si is qui apud te pecuniam deposuerit, bellum inferat patriae, reddasne depositum? non credo: facias enim contra rem publicam, quae debet esse carissima. sic multa quae honesta natura videntur esse, temporibus fiunt non honesta; facere promissa, stare **conventis**, reddere deposita commutata utilitate fiunt non honesta.

Cicero, On Duties III.94

Words

exigo 3 **exegi** = obtain, exact; **de noverca** = "of making advances to his stepmother"; **conventum** 2n = agreement.

Names

Hippolytus 2m = Hippolytus, son of Theseus: his stepmother Phaedra fell in love with him, and when he rejected her, accused him of making advances to her; **Iphigenia** 1f = Iphigenia, daughter of Agamemnon.

135

136. Not only does travelling not necessarily make you feel better: it can often actually make you feel worse.

You're certainly not the only one, Lucilius, to have found out that travel doesn't shake off gloom and depression.

animum debes mutare, non **caelum**. licet vastum traieceris mare, licet, ut ait Vergilius noster "terraeque urbesque recedant," sequentur te, quocumque perveneris, vitia. hoc idem querenti cuidam Socrates ait: "quid miraris nihil tibi peregrinatione prodesse, cum te circumferas? premit te eadem causa quae expulit." quid terrarum iuvare novitas potest? quid cognitio urbium aut locorum? **in irritum cedit** ista **iactatio**. quaeris quare te fuga ista non adiuvet? tecum fugis. onus animi deponendum est: non ante tibi ullus placebit locus. vadis huc illuc, ut excutias **insidens** pondus; quod ipsa **iactatione** incommodius fit, sicut in navi **onera** immota minus urgent, **inaequaliter convoluta** citius eam partem in quam incubuere demergunt. quidquid facis, contra te facis, et motu ipso noces tibi: aegrum enim concutis. at cum istud exemeris malum, omnis mutatio loci iucunda fiet; in ultimas expellaris terras licebit, in quolibet **barbariae** angulo conloceris, hospitalis tibi illa qualiscumque sedes erit.

Seneca, Letter 28

Words

caelum 2n (here) = where you live/where you are; **in irritum cedo** 3 = be in vain; **iactatio iactationis** 3f = rushing about; **insideo** 2 = weigh on; **onera** 3npl (here) = cargo; **inaequaliter convoluta** = "unequally distributed"; **barbaria** 1f = foreign land.

137. There is no need to fear death: in any case, like everything else in the universe, we shall in time return again.

Death cannot harm us: for if we no longer exist after death, what is there that can be harmed?

quod si tanta cupiditas te longioris aevi tenet, cogita nihil eorum quae ab oculis abeunt, et in **rerum naturam** ex qua prodierunt ac mox processura sunt reconduntur, consumi. desinunt ista, non pereunt. et mors, quam pertimescimus et recusamus, intermittit vitam, non eripit; veniet iterum qui nos in lucem reponat dies. aequo animo debet, rediturus, exire. observa **orbem** rerum in se **remeantium**: videbis nihil in hoc mundo exstingui, sed **vicibus** descendere ac surgere. aestas abit, sed alter illam annus adducet; hiems cecidit, referent illam sui menses; solem nox obruit, sed ipsam statim dies abiget. **stellarum iste discursus** quicquid praeterit repetit; pars caeli levatur assidue, pars mergitur. denique finem faciam, si hoc unum adiecero: nec infantes nec pueros nec **mente lapsos** timere mortem, et esse turpissimum si eam securitatem nobis ratio non praestat, ad quam stultitia perducit.

Seneca, Letter 36

Words

rerum natura 1f (here) = the fabric of the universe; **orbis orbis** 3m (here) = round, cycle; **remeo** 1 = return, revert; **vicibus** = in turn; **stellarum iste discursus** = "the wandering stars"; **mente lapsi** 2 mpl = madmen.

138. One should not judge slaves, or any kind of man, by their appearance or occupation.

Our ancestors were right in their treatment of slaves, regarding them as members of the family, giving them rights and honours, as if the household were a tiny state.

"quid ergo? omnes servos **admovebo** mensae meae?" non magis quam omnes liberos. erras si existimas me quosdam quasi sordidioris operae reiecturum, ut (puta) illum **mulionem** et illum **bubulcum**. non **ministeriis** illos aestimabo sed moribus: sibi quisque dat mores, **ministeria** casus assignat. quidam cenent tecum quia digni sunt, quidam ut sint; si quid enim in illis ex sordida **conversatione** servile est, honestiorum **convictus** excutiet. non est, mi Lucili, quod amicum tantum in foro et in curia quaeras: si diligenter attenderis, et domi invenies. saepe bona materia cessat sine artifice: tempta et experire. **quemadmodum** stultus est qui equum empturus non ipsum inspicit sed **stratum** eius ac **frenos**, sic stultissimus est qui hominem aut ex veste aut ex condicione aestimat. "servus est." sed fortasse liber animo. "servus est." hoc illi nocebit? ostende quis non sit: alius libidini servit, alius avaritiae, alius ambitioni, omnes spei, omnes timori.

Seneca, Letter 47

Words

admoveo 2 = invite; **mulio mulionis** 3m = muleteer; **bubulcus** 2m = ploughman; **ministerium** 2n = job; **conversatio conversationis** 3f = association, company; **convictus** 4m = living with, companionship; **quemadmodum** = just as; **stratum** 2n = saddle; **freni** 2mpl = bridle.

139. Rufus is saved from the consequences of an unwise remark by the clemency of the Emperor and the quick thinking of a slave.

In the time of Augustus Caesar, it was not yet the case that what a man said could endanger his life, but it could certainly be damaging.

Rufus, vir ordinis senatorii, inter cenam optaverat ne Caesar salvus rediret ex ea peregrinatione quam parabat. fuerunt qui illa diligenter audirent. ut primum **diluxit**, servus qui cenanti ad pedes steterat, narrat quae inter cenam ebrius dixisset, et hortatur ut Caesarem occupet atque ipse se deferat. usus consilio **descendenti** occurrit et, cum malam mentem habuisse se pridie iurasset, optavit et Caesarem ut ignosceret sibi, rediretque in gratiam secum rogavit. cum dixisset se Caesar facere, "nemo," inquit, "credet te mecum in gratiam redisse, nisi aliquid donaveris," petitque **non fastidiendam summam** et impetravit. Caesar ait: "**mea causa** dabo operam ne umquam tibi irascar!" honeste fecit Caesar, quod ignovit, quod liberalitatem clementiae adiecit. quicumque hoc audierit exemplum, necesse est Caesarem laudet, sed cum ante servum laudaverit. non exspectas ut tibi narrem manumissum, qui hoc fecerit. nec tamen **gratis**: pecuniam pro libertate eius Caesar **numeraverat**!

Seneca, On Benefits III.27

Words

dilucesco 3 diluxi = get light; **descendenti** (dat) = "him (Caesar), as he was going down to the forum"; **non fastidiendam summam** = "a far from negligible sum"; **mea causa** = for my own sake; **gratis** adv = free, for nothing; **numero** 1 (here) = pay.

139

140. Assailing the reputations of those who are beyond reproach is not only wrong, but a waste of effort.

This is what Socrates said when he was in that prison which by his presence he made more honourable than any senate-house:

"qui iste furor, quae ista inimica dis hominibusque natura est **infamare** virtutes et malignis sermonibus sancta violare? si potestis, bonos laudate, si minus, transite; quod si vobis exercere taetram istam licentiam placet, alter in alterum **incursitate**. nam cum in caelum insanitis, non dico sacrilegium facitis, sed operam perditis. praebui ego aliquando **Aristophani** materiam iocorum, tota illa comicorum poetarum manus in me venenatos **sales** suos effudit: illustrata est virtus mea per ea ipsa per quae petebatur; **produci** enim illi et temptari expedit, nec ulli magis intellegunt quanta sit quam qui vires eius lacessendo senserunt: duritia silicis nullis magis quam ferientibus nota est. praebeo me non aliter quam rupes aliqua in **vadoso** mari destituta, quam fluctus non desinunt verberare, nec ideo aut loco eam movent aut per tot aetates crebro incursu suo consumunt. adsilite, facite impetum: ferendo vos vincam. in ea quae firma et inexsuperabilia sunt quidquid incurrit **malo suo** vim suam exercet: proinde quaerite aliquam mollem cedentemque materiam in qua tela vestra figantur."

Seneca, On the Happy Life 27

Words
infamo 1 = denigrate; **incursito** 1 = attack; **sal salis** 3m (here) = wit (literally = salt); **produco** 3 = expose; **vadosus** adj = shallow; **malo suo** = to its own detriment.

Names
Aristophanes Aristophanis 3m = Aristophanes, the comic playwright.

140

141. All nature stops to hear Idas and Astacus sing as they c for the love of Crocale.

Idas the shepherd and Astacus the gardener loved the virgin Crocale.
Both of them were handsome boys, and both fine singers.

    hi, cum terras gravis ureret aestas,
ad gelidos fontes et easdem forte sub ulmos
conveniunt, dulcique parant contendere cantu.
adfuit omne genus pecudum, genus omne ferarum,
et quodcumque vagis altum **ferit** aethera pennis;
convenit umbrosa quicumque sub ilice lentus
pascit oves, Faunusque pater Satyrique bicornes;
adfuerunt sicco **Dryades** pede, **Naiades** udo,
et tenuere suos properantia flumina cursus;
desistunt tremulis incurrere frondibus **Euri**,
altaque per totos fecere silentia montes.
omnia cessabant, neglectaque **pascua** tauri
calcabant; illis etiam certantibus ausa est
daedala nectareos apis intermittere flores.
*   Calpurnius Siculus, II.4*

Words
ferio 4 (here) = beat; **pascua** 2npl = meadows; **calco** 1 = trample.
Names
Dryades Dryadum 3fpl = wood-nymphs; **Naiades Naiadum** 3fpl = water-nymphs; **Eurus** 2m = East wind.

abandoned by Theseus on Naxos, has nowhere to
vengeance before she dies.

r, how I wish that the Athenian ships had never reached
evil man had never come to our house.

nam quo me referam? quali spe, perdita, nitor?
Idaeosne petam montes? a, gurgite lato
discernens ponti truculentum dividit aequor!
an patris auxilium sperem? quemne ipsa reliqui
respersum iuvenem fraterna caede secuta?
coniugis an fido **consoler memet** amore
quine fugit lentos incurvans gurgite remos?
praeterea nullo colitur sola insula tecto,
nec patet egressus pelagi cingentibus undis:
nulla fugae ratio, nulla spes; omnia muta,
omnia sunt deserta, ostentant omnia letum.
non tamen ante mihi languescent **lumina** morte,
nec prius a fesso secedent corpore sensus,
quam iustam a divis exposcam prodita **multam**,
caelestemque fidem postrema comprecor hora.

Catullus LXIV.177

Words

respersus adj = spattered (Ariadne had helped Theseus kill the
Minotaur, her brother); **consolor** 1dep = console; **memet** = **me**; **lumina**
3npl (here) = eyes; **multa** 1f = revenge.

Names

Idaeus adj = of Mount Ida, in Crete.

142

143. There is no sense in worrying: everything in life is ruled by fate.

[The passage is the beginning of Book IV of Manilius's poem on astronomy: he goes on to explain how our characters and lives are governed by astrology.]

quid tam sollicitis vitam consumimus annis
torquemurque metu caecaque cupidine rerum
aeternisque **senes** curis, dum quaerimus, aevum
perdimus et nullo votorum fine beati
victuros agimus semper nec vivimus umquam?
solvite, mortales, animos curasque levate
totque **supervacuis** vitam **deplete** querelis.
fata regunt orbem, certa stant omnia lege:
nascentes morimur, finisque ab origine pendet.
hinc et opes et regna fluunt et, saepius orta,
paupertas, artesque datae moresque **creatis**
et vitia et laudes, damna et **compendia** rerum.
nemo carere dato poterit nec habere negatum
fortunamve suis invitam prendere votis
aut fugere instantem; sors est sua cuique ferenda.

Manilius, IV.1

Words

senes = growing old/old before our time; **victuros agimus** = "we mean to live"; **supervacuus** adj = vain, irrelevant; **depleo** 2 = rid; **creatis** = "when they/we are born"; **compendium** 2n = gain.

144. Catullus explains to a friend that the death of his brother has taken all the joy from his life.

You ask me to write something to console you; I am glad you asked me, because it shows that we are friends:

sed tibi ne mea sint ignota **incommoda, Mani,**
  neu me odisse putes hospitis officium,
accipe, quis **merser** fortunae fluctibus ipse,
  ne amplius a misero dona beata petas.
tempore quo primum vestis mihi tradita pura est,
  iucundum cum aetas florida ver ageret,
multa satis lusi: non est dea nescia nostri,
  quae dulcem curis miscet amaritiem.
sed totum hoc studium luctu fraterna mihi mors
  abstulit. o misero frater adempte mihi,
tu mea, tu moriens, fregisti **commoda,** frater;
  tecum una tota est nostra sepulta domus;
omnia tecum una perierunt gaudia nostra,
  quae tuus in vita dulcis alebat amor.
cuius ego interitu tota de mente fugavi
  haec studia atque omnes delicias animi.
                              Catullus, LXVIII

Words
incommodum 2n = problem; **merso** 1 = immerse, overwhelm;
tempore...pura est: i.e. when Catullus came of age and assumed the
toga virilis; **commodum** 2n (here) = pleasure.
Names
Manius 2m = Manius, Catullus' friend.

145. Dis, god of the Underworld, has carried off Proserpina to be his wife; here he consoles her by showing her what she will gain.

By her words and by her tears that fierce lord was vanquished, and he felt the first stirrings of love. So he dried her tears with his black cloak and tried to soothe her with calming words:

"desine funestis animum, Proserpina, curis
et vano vexare metu. maiora dabuntur
sceptra, nec indigni **taedas** patiere mariti.
ille ego Saturni proles cui **machina rerum**
servit, et immensum tendit per inane potestas.
amissum ne crede **diem**: sunt altera nobis
sidera, sunt orbes alii, lumenque videbis
purius **Elysium**que magis mirabere solem
cultoresque pios. illic pretiosior aetas,
aurea progenies habitat, semperque tenemus
quod superi meruere semel. nec mollia desunt
prata tibi: **Zephyris** illic melioribus **halant**
perpetui flores, quos nec tua protulit **Aetna**.
est etiam lucis **arbos** praedives opacis,
fulgentes viridi ramos curvata metallo.
haec tibi sacra datur, fortunatumque tenebis
autumnum, et fulvis semper **ditabere** pomis."

Claudian, The Rape of Proserpina II.277

Words

taeda 1f = marriage; **machina rerum** = the world; **dies** (here) = light; **halo** 1 = be fragrant; **arbos** = **arbor**; **dito** 1 = enrich.

Names

Elysius adj = Elysian: of the Elysian fields, the "heaven" of the Underworld; **Zephyrus** 2m = West wind; **Aetna** 1f = Mount Etna, in Sicily where Proserpina came from.

146. Why invite death by going to war? Tibullus advocates a quiet life in the country.

Who was the man who invented the sword? What a cruel man, a truly iron man, he must have been! Then the way was open for slaughter and for war, and a quicker way to die.

quis furor est atram bellis **accersere** mortem?
  imminet et tacito clam venit illa pede.
non seges est infra, non **vinea** culta, sed audax
  Cerberus et **Stygiae navita** turpis **aquae**;
illic **pertusis**que genis ustoque capillo
  errat ad obscuros pallida turba lacus.
quin potius laudandus hic est quem, prole parata,
  occupat in parva pigra senecta casa!
ipse suas sectatur oves, at filius agnos,
  et calidam fesso comparat uxor aquam.
sic ego sim, liceatque caput **candescere** canis,
  temporis et prisci facta referre senem.
interea pax arva colat: pax candida primum
  duxit araturos sub iuga curva boves;
pax aluit vites et **sucos condidit** uvae,
  funderet ut nato **testa** paterna merum;
pace **bidens vomer**que nitent, at tristia duri
  militis in tenebris occupat arma **situs**.
Tibullus, I.10

Words

accerso 3 = invite; **vinea** 1f = vineyard; **navita** 1m = **nauta**; **pertusus** adj = torn; **quin** = surely; **candesco** 3 = go white; **sucus** 2m = juice; **condo** 3 **condidi** (here) = store up; **testa** 1f = jar; **bidens bidentis** 3m = hoe; **vomer vomeris** 3m = ploughshare; **situs** 4m = rust.

Names

Cerberus 2m = Cerberus, the dog who guards the Underworld; **Stygia aqua** 1f = the waters of the Styx, one of the rivers of the Underworld.

147. A vision of Rome personified terrifies Caesar and his men as they are about to precipitate Civil War; Caesar protests that it is not his wish.

[Lucan has been outlining the causes of the Civil War between Caesar and Pompey. His narrative begins, below, when Caesar has reached the river Rubicon, beyond which he was not legally allowed to lead his army.]

iam gelidos Caesar cursu superaverat Alpes,
ingentique animo **motus** bellumque futurum
ceperat. ut ventum est parvi Rubiconis ad undas,
lugens visa duci Patriae trepidantis imago,
clara per obscuram vultu maestissima noctem,
caesarie lacera nudisque adstare lacertis
et gemitu permixta loqui: "quo tenditis ultra?
quo fertis mea signa, viri? si iure venitis,
si cives, **huc usque licet.**" tunc perculit horror
membra ducis: **riguere** comae, gressusque coercens
languor in extrema tenuit vestigia ripa.
mox ait: "o magnae qui moenia prospicis urbis
Tarpeia de **rupe Tonans, Phrygiique** Penates
Vestalesque foci, summique o numinis instar,
Roma, fave coeptis: non te **furialibus** armis
persequor; en, adsum victor terraque marique,
Caesar, ubique tuus **(liceat modo, nunc quoque)** miles.
ille erit, ille nocens, qui me tibi fecerit hostem."

Lucan, Civil War I.183

Words

motus 4m = rebellion; **caesaries** 5f = hair; **huc...licet** = "this is as far as you can go"; **rigesco** 3 **rigui** = stand on end; **languor languoris** 3m (here) = irresolution, doubt; **furialis** adj = hostile; **liceat...quoque** = "now also, if allowed to be so".

Names

Tarpeia rupes f = the Tarpeian Rock, in Rome; **Tonans Tonantis** m = the Thunderer, title of Jupiter; **Phrygius** adj = Trojan; **Vestalis** adj = of the goddess Vesta.

148. Claudian reflects on the uneventful but happy life of an old countryman from near Verona.

[Beginning of the poem.]

felix, qui propriis aevum transegit in arvis;
  ipsa domus puerum quem videt, ipsa senem;
qui, baculo nitens in qua **reptavit** harena,
  unius numerat saecula longa casae.
illum non vario traxit fortuna tumultu,
  nec bibit ignotas mobilis hospes aquas.
non freta **mercator** tremuit, non **classica** miles,
  non rauci **lites** pertulit ille fori.
indocilis rerum, vicinae nescius urbis,
  aspectu fruitur liberiore poli.
frugibus alternis, non consule, computat annum;
  autumnum pomis, ver sibi flore notat.
ingentem meminit parvo qui **germine** quercum
  aequaevumque videt consenuisse nemus;
proxima cui nigris Verona remotior **Indis**,
  Benacumque putat **litora Rubra lacum**.
erret et extremos alter **scrutetur Hiberos**:
  plus habet hic vitae, plus habet ille viae.

                   Claudian, Epigram II

Words

repto 1 = crawl; **mercator** = "as a merchant"; **classicum** 2n = trumpet;
lis litis 3f = quarrel; **germen germinis** 3n = shoot, sapling; **aequaevus**
adj = of the same age; **scrutor** 1dep = search out, visit.

Names

Indi 2pml = Indians; **Benacus lacus** m = Lake Garda, near Verona;
litora Rubra npl = the Red Sea; **Hiberi** 2mpl = Spaniards.

149. **War amongst the bees: despite the epic nature of their encounters, they can soon be stopped by the beekeeper.**

But sometimes they go out to battle, for fierce strife often arises between two kings [i.e. queens].

continuoque animos **vulgi** et trepidantia bello
corda licet longe **praesciscere**: namque **morantes**
Martius ille **aeris** rauci canor **increpat**, et vox
auditur fractos sonitus imitata tubarum;
tum trepidae inter se coeunt **pennisque coruscant**
spiculaque **exacuunt rostris** aptantque lacertos
et circa regem atque ipsa ad praetoria densae
miscentur magnisque vocant clamoribus hostem.
ergo ubi **ver** nactae **sudum** camposque patentes,
erumpunt portis; concurritur, aethere in alto
fit sonitus, magnum mixtae glomerantur in orbem
praecipitesque cadunt; non densior aere grando,
nec de concusso tantum pluit ilice **glandis**.
ipsi per medias acies insignibus alis
ingentes animos angusto in pectore versant,
usque adeo obnixi non cedere dum gravis aut hos
aut hos versa fuga victor dare terga subegit.
hi motus animorum atque haec certamina tanta
pulveris exigui iactu compressa quiescent.

Virgil, Georgics IV.69

Words
vulgus 2n (here) = the ordinary bees; **praescisco** 3 = anticipate, know
in advance; **morantes** = those who are slow to come out; **aes aeris** 3n
(here) = trumpet; **increpo** 1 = urge on; **pennis corusco** 1 = flap wings;
spiculum 2n = sting; **exacuo** 3 = sharpen; **rostrum** 2n = beak; **ver
sudum** = "a fine spring day"; **glans glandis** 3f = acorn; **ipsi** = the
kings; **usque...obnixi** = absolutely determined.
Names
Martius adj = of Mars: warlike.

149

150. Praise of the greatness of Rome from one of the last poets of the Roman Empire on leaving the city to return to his home in Gaul.

I kissed the gates I had to leave; unwillingly my feet crossed the holy threshold. I wept and begged forgiveness and, as far as I could through my tears, offered this hymn of praise:

"exaudi, regina tui pulcherrima mundi,
  inter sidereos Roma recepta polos,
exaudi, genetrix hominum genetrixque deorum:
  non procul a caelo per tua templa sumus;
te canimus semperque, sinent dum fata, canemus;
  sospes nemo potest immemor esse tui.
obruerint citius scelerata oblivia solem,
  quam tuus ex nostro corde recedat honos.
nam solis radiis aequalia **munera tendis**,
  qua circumfusus fluctuat Oceanus.
volvitur ipse tibi, qui continet omnia, Phoebus,
  eque tuis ortos in tua condit equos.
te non flammigeris **Libye** tardavit harenis,
  non armata suo reppulit **Ursa** gelu:
quantum vitalis natura tetendit in axes,
  tantum virtuti **pervia** terra tuae.
fecisti patriam diversis gentibus unam:
  profuit iniustis te dominante capi.
dumque offers victis proprii **consortia** iuris,
  urbem fecisti quod prius orbis erat."

           Rutilius Namatianus, On his Return I.47

Words

sospes sospitis adj = safe; **obruo** 3 **obrui** = overwhelm, overtake; **munera tendis** = "you spread your gifts/extend your benefits"; **pervius** adj = accessible; **consortia** 3npl (here) = share.

Names

Libye (nom) = Africa; **Ursa** 1f = the North (literally the Great Bear constellation).

a/ab
absum
ac/atque
accido
accipio
ad
adhuc
adiuvo
adsum
adventus
aedificium
aedifico
aequus
aestas
aetas
ager
ago
agricola
aliquis
alius
alter
altus
ambulo
amicitia
amicus
amo
animus
annus
ante
antea
antequam
antiquus
aperio
appareo
appello
appropinquo
apud

aqua
argentum
arma
ars
arx
ascendo
at
audeo
audio
auris
aurum
aut
autem
auxilium
barbarus
bellum
bene
bibo
bonus
brevis
cado (-cid-)
caedo (-cid-)
caelum
campus
cano
capio (-cip-)
captivus
caput
carmen
carus
castra
causa
celer
celeritas
celo
cena
ceno

centurio
certe
cibus
circa
circum
civis
clamo
clamor
[prae]clarus
coepi
cogo
cognosco
collis
comes
complures
confido
conor
consilium
conspicio
constituo
consul
contendo
contra
copia
copiae
corpus
cotidie
cras
credo
crudelis
culpa
cum
cupiditas
cupidus
cupio
cur
cura.

curo	enim	fortitudo
curro	eo (VB)	fortuna
custodio	eo (ADV)	frater
custos	epistula	frustra
damno	eques	fuga
de	equus	fugio
debeo	erro	gens
dedo	et	gero
deditio	etiam	gladius
defendo	etsi	gloria
dein[de]	excito	gravis
deleo	exercitus	habeo
descendo	exspecto	habito
desero	extra	[h]arena
despero	extremus	hasta
deus	fabula	haud
dico	facilis	herba
dies	facio (-fic-)	heri
difficilis	fama	hic
discedo	fatum	hiems
disco	femina	hinc
diu	fero	hodie
divido	ferrum	homo
do	fessus	honos
doceo	fidelis	hora
dolor	fides	hortor
dominus	filia	hortus
domus	filius	hospes
donec	finis	hostis
donum	fio	huc
dubito	firmus	humus
dubius	flamma	iaceo
duco	flecto	iacio (-ic-)
dum	flos	iam
durus	flumen	ibi
dux	fluo	idem
e/ex	fortasse	igitur
ecce	forte	ignis
ego	fortis	ignoro

ignotus	itaque	maritus
ille	iter	mater
illic	iterum	medius
illinc	iubeo	memini
illuc	iustus	meus
impedimenta	iuvenis	miles
impedio	iuvo	minor (VB)
imperator	labor (NOUN)	miror
imperium	labor (VB)	miser
impero	laboro	mitto
in	lacrima	modo
incendo	lacus	modus
incipio	laetus	moneo
inde	laudo	mons
inferior	legatus	morior
ingens	legio	mors
inimicus	lego	mos
iniquus	levis	moveo
initium	libens	mox
iniuria	liber (ADJ)	multitudo
inopia	liberi	multo/multum
inquam	libero	multus
instituo	locus	murus
insula	longus	nam[que]
intellego	loquor	nato/no
inter	ludo	nauta
interea	ludus	navigo
interficio	lumen	navis
interim	luna	ne
intra	magis	-ne
intro	magistratus	nec/neque
invenio	magnitudo	necesse
ipse	magnopere	neco
ira	magnus	nego
irascor	malo	nemo
iratus	malus	nescio
is	maneo	neuter
iste	manus	nihil/nil
ita	mare	nimis/nimium

nisi/ni	ora	populus
nobilis	oratio	porta
nolo/noli	orator	porto
nomen	oro	possum
non	osculum	post
nondum	ostendo	postea
nonne	paene	postquam
nonnullus	pareo	postremo
nos	paro	postridie
nosco	pars	potestas
noster	parvus	praeda
notus	passus	praemium
novus	pater	praeter
nox	patior	praeterea
nullus	patria	premo
num	paucus	primo/primum
numerus	paulatim	princeps
numquam	paulisper	priusquam
nunc	paulo/paulum	pro
nuntio	pauper	proelium
nuntius	pax	proficiscor
nuper	pecunia	prohibeo
ob	pedes	prope
obtineo	pello	propter
occasio	per	provincia
occido (kill)	perfidia	prudens
occupo	perfidus	prudentia
oculus	pereo	puella
odi	periculum	puer
odium	persuadeo	pugna
offero	pes	pugno
officium	peto	pulcher
olim	-plector	puto
omen	pleo	qualis
omnis	plurimus	quam
oppidum	plus	quamquam
opprimo	poena	quando
oppugno	poeno	quantus
opus	pons	-que

qui	saxum	statuo
quia	scelestus	sto
quidam	scelus	sub
quidem	scio	subito
quin	scribo	sum
quis	scutum	sumo
quisquam	se	summus
quisque	sed	super
quo	sedeo	superbus
quod	semper	superior
quominus	senator	supero
quomodo	senatus	suscipio
quoniam	senex	sustineo
quoque	sentio	suus
quot	sequor	talis
quotie[n]s	sermo	tam
rapio	servo	tamen
recipio	servus	tandem
redeo	si	tantus
regina	sic	tego
regnum	sicut[i]	telum
rego	signum	templum
relinquo	silentium	tempto
reliquus	silva	tempus
res	similis	teneo (-tin-)
res publica	simul	tergum
resisto	simulac	terra
respondeo	sine	terreo
rex	socius	timeo
ripa	sol	timor
rogo	solum (NOUN)	tollo
rumpo	solum (ADV)	tot
rursus	solus	totie[n]s
sacer	somnus	totus
saepe	soror	traho
saevus	specto	trans
sagitta	spero	tristis
sanguis	spes	triumphus
satis	statim	tu

tuba	vasto	victoria
tum	vastus	video
turbo	-ve	videor
tutus	veho	villa
tuus	vel	vinco
ubi	venio	vinum
ullus	ventus	vir
ultimus	ver	virtus
umquam	verbum	vis
unda	vero	vires
unde	verto	vita
undique	verum	vito
urbs	verus	vivo
ut[i]	vesper	vivus
uterque	vester	vix
utilis	vestis	voco
utor	veto	volo (velle)
utrum (...an)	vetus	vos
uxor	vexo	vox
vacuus	via	vulnero
validus	vicinus	vulnus
vallum	victor	vultus

adimo 3 ademi ademptum	take away
casus 4m	chance; disaster
-cedo 3 -cessi -cessum	go [uncomp. = yield]
civitas civitatis 3f	state
claudo 3 clausi clausum	close
committo 3 commisi commissum	entrust; join (battle)
conditor conditoris 3m	founder
conspectus 4m	view
desino 3 desi[v]i desitum	cease
dignitas dignitatis 3f	dignity
dimico 1	fight (to a finish)
evado 3 evasi evasum	escape
explorator exploratoris 3m	scout
fames famis 3f	hunger
frango 3 fregi fractum	break
fugo 1	rout
fundo 3 fudi fusum	pour; shed; rout
-gredior 3dep -gressus	go
honestus adj	honourable
invidia 1f	envy; hatred
longe adv	far
minus adv	less
obsideo 2 obsedi obsessum	beseige
orbis orbis 3m (terrarum)	globe; world
perdo 3 perdidi perditum	destroy; lose
posco 3 poposci	demand; ask
quasi conj	as if
queror 3dep questus sum	complain
quicumque quaecumque quodcumque	whoever/whatever
quondam adv	once
reddo 3 reddidi redditum	give back
sepelio 4 sepelivi sepultum	bury
servio 4 (+ dat)	serve; am a slave
suadeo 2 suasi suasum (+dat)	urge
supplicium 2n	punishment
tantum adv	only
tracto 1	treat

triumpho 1	celebrate a triumph
utrimque adv	from/on both sides

Word List 2 (Passages 6 - 10)

ait	[s]he says/said
amens amentis adj	senseless, mad
aro 1	plough
auctor auctoris 3m	doer, person responsible
aura 1f	breeze
caelestis adj	heavenly
crus cruris 3n	leg
(ex)cutio 3 -cussi -cussum	shake (out)
fecundus adj	fertile
ferus adj	wild
fons fontis 3m	spring
fulmen fulminis 3n	lightning; thunderbolt
immanis adj	huge; monstrous
inermis adj	unarmed
iungo 3 iunxi iunctum	join (trans)
limen liminis 3n	threshold
liquidus adj	clear
luctus 4m	grief
membrum 2n	limb
metus 4m	fear
monstrum 2n	monster
mortalis adj	mortal
nata 1f / natus 2m	daughter/son
onus oneris 3n	burden
os oris 3n	mouth; face
pallor palloris 3m	paleness
pius adj	good; dutiful
plenus adj	full
pondus ponderis 3n	weight
salus salutis 3f	safety
saluto 1	greet
sceleratus adj	wicked
sero 3 sevi satum	sow (seed)

sidus sideris 3n	star
sollicito 1	agitate, trouble
stultus adj	foolish, stupid
subitus adj	sudden
tollo 3 sustuli sublatum	raise; take (away)
turpis adj	ugly; disgraceful
vigor vigoris 3m	strength

Word List 3 (Passages 11 - 15)

aegre adv	with difficulty
aquila 1f	eagle; standard
certior[em] facio 3 feci factum	inform
circumvenio 4 -veni -ventum	surround
commeatus 4m	provisions
condicio condicionis 3f	condition; (pl) terms
consulo 3 consului consultum (+dat)	consult interests of
deficio 3 defeci defectum	fail; desert
equitatus 4m	cavalry
expugno 1	take by storm
facultas facultatis 3f	opportunity
fere adv	about
fines finium 3mpl	territory
fossa 1f	ditch
idoneus adj	suitable
impedimenta 2npl	baggage
impetro 1	get one's wish
impetus 4m	attack
incolumis adj	unharmed
instruo 3 instruxi instructum	draw up; order
munio 4	fortify
noctu adv	by night
nostri 2mpl	our men
ordo ordinis 3m	rank, order
passim adv	everywhere
praecipito 1	throw down
prius adv	earlier, first
proinde adv	therefore

proximus adj	nearest, next
saluti esse (+dat)	to bring safety to
spatium 2n	space, interval
statio stationis 3f	position, post
subsidium 2n	help; reserves
subvenio 4 -veni -ventum (+dat)	come to help
sui 2mpl	his men
tumulus 2m	small hill
una (cum)	together (with)
usui esse (+dat)	to be of use to
vereor 2dep veritus sum	fear

Word List 4 (Passages 16 - 20)

aditus 4m	approach, way in
aes aeris 3n	bronze; thing of bronze
aether aetheris 3m	air, sky
ardor ardoris 3m	burning; love; lover
aspicio 3 aspexi aspectum	see
castus adj	chaste
colloquium 2n	meeting; conversation
coniunx coniugis 3c	husband/wife
creber crebra crebrum adj	frequent; repeated
crinis crinis 3m	hair
dextra 1f	right hand
fidus adj	faithful
fletus 4m	weeping
galea 1f	helmet
geminus adj	double, twin
genetrix genetricis 3f	mother
heros herois 3m	hero
imitor 1dep	imitate
insto 1 institi	press on
iuventus iuventutis 3f	young men
moenia moenium 3npl	defences
nebula 1f	cloud
numen numinis 3n	god; divine will
patrius adj	of one' father

pectus pectoris 3n	chest, breast
praebeo 2	provide; offer
preces precum 3fpl	prayers
precor 1dep	pray
protinus adv	immediately
pudet 2 impers	it shames
pulvis pulveris 3m	dust
puppis puppis 3f	ship
resto 1 restiti	stay, stop
ruo 3 rui rutum	rush; collapse
sors sortis 3f	lot, fate
sterno 3 stravi stratum	lay low
subeo subire subii subitum	go under/up to
tremo 3 tremui	tremble (at)
urgeo 2	press on
volo 1	fly

Word List 5 (Passages 21 - 25)

adipiscor 3dep adeptus sum	obtain
adorior 4dep adortus sum	attack
adversus + acc	against
aequalis adj	contemporary
arbitror 1dep	think
armatus adj/2m	armed/armed man
bello 1	wage war
bona 2npl	goods, property
causa 1f	cause, reason; case
causam dico 3 dixi dictum	plead a case
ceterus adj	rest, other
circumdo 1 -dedi -datum	surround
clam adv	secretly
cunctus adj	whole; pl. all
diutius adv	any longer
dono 1	present
exitus 4m	way out
experior 4dep expertus sum	try out; prove
foris foris 3f	door

ianua 1f	door
immineo 2 (+dat)	threaten
lateo 2	lie hidden
litterae 1fpl	letter
memor adj (+gen)	remembering
munus muneris 3n	gift
obsidio obsidionis 3f	siege
ops opis 3f	help; pl. resources
perpetuus adj	continual
praesidium 2n	garrison, bodyguard
praesidio esse (+dat)	to protect
pristinus adj	original; previous
propere adv	quickly
reus 2m	defendant
revertor 3dep reverti	go back
sacra 2npl	sacred things
scilicet adv	presumably; of course
[dis]solvo 3 -solvi -solutum	loosen; break up
talentum 2n	talent (of money)
venenum 2n	poison
violo 1	violate, defile

Word List 6 (Passages 26 - 30)

absens adj	absent
aeger aegra aegrum adj	sick
agnosco 3 agnovi agnitum	recognise
alo 3 alui al[i]tum	nourish
arva 2npl	fields, land
casa 1f	cottage
cerno 3 crevi cretum	see
confiteor 2dep confessus sum	admit
diva 1f/ divus 2m	goddess/god
divitiae 1fpl	riches
exsul exsulis 3c	an exile
ferio 4	strike
fleo 2 flevi fletum	weep
formido formidinis 3f	fear

gemitus 4m	groan[ing]
[in]haereo 2 -haesi -haesum	stick to; cling to
lacertus 2m	arm
lar laris 3m	household god; home
lassus adj	weary
maestus adj	sad
misceo 2 miscui mixtum	mix; combine
mollis adj	soft, gentle
nescioquis/nescioquid	someone/something; some
nitidus adj	bright
orior 4dep ortus sum	arise
otium 2n	peace; leisure
pascor 3dep pastus sum	feed on
pecus pecoris 3n	herd, flock
pietas pietatis 3f	goodness; duty
placeo 2 (+dat)	please
plaustrum 2n	cart
[ne]queo -quire -qui[v]i -quitum	am [un]able
rus ruris 3n	countryside
stella 1f	star
studium 2n	study; enthusiasm
[ad]suesco 3 -suevi -suetum	be/become accustomed to
trepido 1	panic; worry
umerus 2m	shoulder
[a]vello 3 - velli/-vulsi -vulsum	tear [away]
vincio 4 vinxi vinctum	tie, bind

Word List 7 (Passages 31 - 35)

acer acris acre adj	keen, fierce, bitter
acies 5f	battle-line
apertus adj	open
auctoritas auctoritatis 3f	influence
augeo 2 auxi auctum	increase (trans)
avaritia 1f	greed
avidus adj	keen; greedy
caecus adj	blind; unseen
caedes caedis 3f	killing, slaughter

certamen certaminis 3n	contest; battle
ceterum conj	but
cohors cohortis 3f	cohort
comminus adv	at close quarters
coniuratio coniurationis 3f	conspiracy
cunctor 1dep	delay, hesitate
decerno 3 decrevi decretum	decide; decree
desisto 3 destiti	cease
dolus 2m	trick, ambush
existimo 1	think
facinus facinoris 3n	evil deed
fretus adj (+abl)	relying on
genus generis 3n	kind; family
gratia 1f	favour; influence
ignavia 1f	cowardice; laziness
infestus adj	hostile
latus lateris 3n	side; flank
libido libidinis 3f	lust
metuo 3 metui	fear
moror 1dep	delay
par paris adj	equal; similar
pilum 2n	spear
plerique adj	most, very many
porro adv	forward; moreover
praecipio 3 -cepi -ceptum (+dat)	instruct
pravus adj	wicked
qua conj	where
tametsi conj	although
usquam adv	anywhere
veteranus 2m	experienced soldier

Word List 8 (Passages 36 - 40)

amplexus 4m	embrace
anguis anguis 3c	snake
ardeo 2 arsi arsum	burn; fall in love
bracchium 2n	arm
collum 2n	neck

164

cornu 4n	horn; wing of army
cresco 3 crevi	grow
densus adj	thick, dense
draco draconis 3m	snake
facies 5f	face
forma 1f	form; beauty
genu 4n	knee
imago imaginis 3f	image, likeness; ghost
interdum adv	sometimes
latebra 1f	hiding place
litus litoris 3n	shore
marmor marmoris 3n	marble; sea
mergo 3 mersi mersum	immerse; plunge
[per]mulceo 2 -mulsi -mulsum	soothe; stroke
nemus nemoris 3n	wood
nequiquam adv	in vain
nudus adj	naked
occasus 4m	setting; west
ortus 4m	rising; east
palma 1f	palm; hand
pariter adv	equally; together
penna 1f	feather; wing
piget 2impers	it causes regret
porrigo 3 porrexi porrectum	stretch out
probo 1	test; approve of
serpo 3 serpsi	creep
sinus 4n	curve; bay; lap
sitis sitis 3f	thirst
soleo 2semi-dep solitus sum	am accustomed
[de]spicio 3 -spexi -spectum	look [down]
[ad]stupeo 2 -stupui	am amazed
tango 3 tetigi tactum	touch
tendo 3 tetendi tentum	stretch out
valeo 2	am well; am able
virgo virginis 3f	maiden, virgin

adulescens adulescentis 3m	young man
aedes aedis 3f	building; temple
amnis amnis 3m	river
artifex artificis 3n	artist, craftsman
belua 1f	beast, monster
carcer carceris 3m	prison
classis classis 3f	fleet
colo 3 colui cultum	cultivate; worship
consensus 4m	agreement
contentus adj	satisfied
crudelitas crudelitatis 3f	cruelty
cruor cruoris 3m	blood
desum deesse defui	fail; am missing
[in]flammo 1	set on fire; inflame
ignominia 1f	disgrace
iucundus adj	pleasant
lacesso 3 lacessivi lacessitum	provoke
mature adv	early; quickly
natio nationis 3f	nation
-ne ... an ...	whether ... or ...
nefarius adj	wicked
negotium 2n	business
nequaquam adv	in no way
nequitia 1f	wickedness
potius adv (quam)	rather (than)
praedo praedonis 3m	pirate, robber
praefectus 2m	commander
praesum praeesse praefui (+dat)	am in command of
quiesco 3 quievi quietum	rest; am quiet
ratio rationis 3f	reason; method
recuso 1	refuse
religio religionis 3f	piety; holiness
repente adv	suddenly
sedes sedis 3f	seat; place; residence
servitus servitutis 3f	slavery
simulacrum 2n	image; statue; ghost
singularis adj	remarkable

vehementer adv	strongly, violently
voluntas voluntatis 3f	will

Word List 10 (Passages 46 - 50)

abdo 3 abdidi abditum	hide
aeternus adj	eternal
aper apri 2m	wild boar
aptus adj	suitable
asper aspera asperum adj	rough; harsh
ater atra atrum adj	black; dark
bellus adj	pretty
cantus 4m	song; magic spell
crimen criminis 3n	accusation; crime
displiceo 2 (+dat)	displease
exemplum 2n	example
formosus adj	handsome; beautiful
humanus adj	human
idcirco adv	therefore
iuro 1	swear
laedo 3 laesi laesum	hurt
[re]levo 1	lift; relieve
licet 2impers/conj + subj	it is allowed/although
niger nigra nigrum adj	black
pecco 1	do wrong
propero 1	hurry
quaero 3 quaesivi quaesitum	seek; ask
quisquis quidquid	whoever, whatever
requies requietis 3f	rest
rusticus adj	rustic; uncouth
salvus adj	safe
sanctus adj	holy
tectum 2n	roof; house
tenebrae 1fpl	darkness
tenuis adj	thin; slender
tepidus adj	warm
torqueo 2 torsi tortum	twist; torture
torus 2m	bed

turba 1f	crowd
usus 4m	use; advantage
utinam + subj	would that!
vallis vallis 3f	valley
velum 2n	sail
votum 2n	vow; prayer
voveo 2 vovi votum	vow

Word List 11 (Passages 51 - 60)

agger aggeris 3m	rampart, bank
agmen agminis 3n	column
angustus adj	narrow; difficult
animadverto 3 -verti -versum	notice
arbor arboris 3f	tree
circiter adv/prep + acc	about
citra adv/prep + acc	on this side (of)
consentio 4 -sensi -sensum	agree
conspicor 1dep	notice
consuetudo consuetudinis 3f	custom
deligo 3 delegi delectum	choose
demum adv	finally
despicio 3 -spexi -spectum	despise
dexter dextra dextrum adj	right
diripio 3 -ripui -reptum	plunder
egregius adj	outstanding
exiguus adj	small
fas n indecl	right
ignosco 3 ignovi (+dat)	forgive
iuxta (+acc)	near, next to
mando 1	entrust
meridies 5f	midday
nanciscor 3dep nactus sum	obtain
ne ... quidem	not even
neu/neve conj	and not
obses obsidis 3c	hostage
obviam adv (+dat)	to meet
occurro 3 -curri -cursum (+dat)	meet

palam adv	openly
peritus adj	skilled
plebs plebis 3f	common people
potior 4dep (+gen/abl)	get possession of
praeficio 3 -feci -fectum	put in command
procul adv	far
propterea adv	therefore; for this reason
quin conj	that; from
reperio 4 repperi repertum	find
res frumentaria f	corn supply
sin conj	but if
sinister sinistra sinistrum adj	left
sive/seu ... sive/seu ...	whether ... or ...
stringo 3 strinxi strictum	draw (sword)
supersum superesse superfui	survive; remain
suspicor 1dep	suspect
temere adv	rashly, ill-advisedly
trado 3 tradidi traditum	hand over
tribunus 2m	officer
usque ad (+acc)	right up to
valetudo valetudinis 3f	health
vigilia 1f	watch (of the night)

Word List 12 (Passages 61 - 70)

aequor aequoris 3n	sea
alveus 2m	channel; river
amor amoris 3m	love
anima 1f	breath; life; soul
artus 4m	limb
astrum 2n	star
axis axis 3m	sky; pole
capilli 2mpl	hair
cautus/incautus adj	careful/careless
cavus adj	hollow
cinis cineris 3m	ashes
currus 4m	chariot
dignus	worthy; deserved

doctus adj	learned
ensis ensis 3m	sword
fallo 3 fefelli falsum	deceive
fluctus 4m	wave
freta 2npl	straits; sea
gena 1f	cheek
hostia 1f	(sacrificial) victim
laevus adj	left
lenis adj	gentle
lux lucis 3f	light; day
maereo 2	grieve
mane adv	in the morning
mensa 1f	table
mereo 2	deserve
mirus adj	amazing
mora 1f	delay
nefas n indecl	wrong
nimius adj	excessive
nubes nubis 3f	cloud
opacus adj	dark
os ossis 3n	bone
paveo 2	be afraid
pavidus adj	fearful
pontus 2m	sea
quamvis conj	although
ratis ratis 3f	ship
remus 2m	oar
rogus 2m	funeral pyre
scopulus 2m	rock
-silio 4 -silui -sultum	jump
sino 3 sivi situm	allow
succurro 3 -curri -cursum (+dat)	come to help of
surgo 3 surrexi surrectum	rise
tellus telluris 3f	land; earth
tempestas tempestatis 3f	storm
vinc[u]lum 2n	chain; fastening
viridis adj	green

adicio 3 adieci adiectum	add
ambo adj	both
benignus adj	kind
celebro 1	celebrate
censeo 2	give one's opinion
comparo 1	obtain; get ready
curia 1f	senate-house
epulae 1fpl	feast
extemplo adv	immediately
ferme adv	about, almost
ferox ferocis adj	fierce
fido 3 semi-dep fisus sum (+dat)	trust; rely on
fluvius 2m	river
grando grandinis 3f	hail
gratus adj	welcome; grateful
haurio 4 hausi haustum	drain; drink
iaculum 2n	spear
ictus adj	struck
ignarus adj	ignorant
imber imbris 3m	rain
inceptum 2n	attempt
intervallum 2n	space; interval
iugum 2n	yoke; ridge
letum 2n	death
lictor lictoris 3m	bodyguard
magister magistri 2m	master
minuo 3 minui minutum	diminish
muto 1	change
orno 1	decorate; equip
parumper adv	for a short time
poculum 2n	cup
poto 1 potavi potatum/potum	drink
pretium 2n	price
proditio proditionis 3f	betrayal
quies quietis 3f	rest; sleep
quoad conj	as far as; as long as
receptus 4m	retreat

risus 4m	laugh
rudis adj	inexperienced
saltus 4m	pass
saucius adj	wounded
segnis adj	slow; reluctant
sententia 1f	opinion
spectaculum 2n	sight
sperno 3 sprevi spretum	reject
tenus (+gen/abl)	up to
traicio 3 traieci traectum	take across; cross
turma 1f	squadron
ultra (+acc) (ulterior adj)	beyond (further)
ultor ultoris 3m	avenger

Word List 14 (Passages 81 - 90)

aliter adv	otherwise
arcus 4m	bow
armenta 2npl	cattle
cingo 3 cinxi cinctum	surround, encircle
coma 1f	hair
cruentus adj	bloody
daps dapis 3f	feast
dives divitis adj	rich
doleo 2	grieve
domo 1 domui domitum	tame
dulcis adj	sweet; pleasant
dummodo conj	provided that
ei interj	oh! alas!
en interj	look!
ergo adv	therefore
exerceo 2	train
facundus adj	eloquent
felix felicis adj	fortunate, happy
flo 1	blow
forsitan adv	perhaps
frigus frigoris 3n	cold
furtim adv	stealthily

gaudeo 2 semi-dep gavisus sum	rejoice
heu interj	alas!
improbus adj	wicked; persistent
iuvenca 1f/iuvencus 2m	cow/bullock
lex legis 3f	law
mens mentis 3f	mind
merus 2m	wine
nempe adv	certainly
nix nivis 3f	snow
opto 1	wish for; choose
palus paludis 3f	marsh
parco 3 peperci parsum (+dat)	spare; cease
pecudes pecudum 3fpl	cattle; flocks
pingo 3 pinxi pictum	paint, depict
praetereo -ire -ii -itum	pass, go by
prodo 3 prodidi proditum	betray
querel[l]a 1f	complaint
recens recentis adj	new; recent
saeculum 2n	generation; century
semel adv	once
taurus 2m	bull
temerarius adj	rash; thoughtless
tener tenera tenerum adj	tender
tepeo 2	be warm; be in love
vates vatis 3m	poet; prophet
velut[i] adv	like, as
virga 1f	stick
vulgus 2n	crowd; common people

Word List 15 (Passages 91 - 100)

accedo 3 accessi accessum	go to; be added
aliquando adv	some time
aliquantum adv	a good deal
ara 1f	altar
arcesso 3 arcessivi arcessitum	summon
cliens clientis 3m	client
comitium 2n	assembly

173

conscius adj	aware of; complicit
contio contionis 3f	meeting; speech
discrimen discriminis 3n	difference; crisis
dormio 4	sleep
equidem	I myself; indeed
etenim	for; in fact
fructus 4m	fruit; gain
fundus 2m	farm
furtum 2n	theft
hospitium 2n	hospitality; inn
integer integra integrum adj	whole
intersum interesse interfui	be between; take part in
iudex iudicis 3m	judge
iudico 1	judge
latro latronis 3m	robber
latus adj	wide
maiores maiorum 3mpl	ancestors
memoro 1	mention; say
misericordia 1f	mercy
monstro 1	show
nascor 3dep natus sum	am born
neglego 3 neglexi neglectum	neglect
occultus adj	hidden; secret
omnino adv	at all
oportet 2impers	it is right
placo 1	placate
posterus adj (posteri 2mpl)	next, later (posterity)
pre[he]ndo 3 pre[he]ndi pre[he]nsum	get hold of
profecto adv	certainly
proprius adj	one's own
quivis quaevis quodvis	any at all
rectus adj	right; straight
rostra 2 npl	rostrum
sero adv	late
spiritus 4m	breath; spirit
spolio 1	despoil
studeo 2 (+dat)	am keen on; study
stupesco 3 stupui	am amazed at
testimonium 2n	evidence

testis testis 3m	witness
trucido 1	slaughter
universi 2mpl	all, everyone
vagor 1dep	wander

Word List 16 (Passages 101 - 110)

aevum 2n	age; life
antrum 2n	cave
aro 1	plough
avis avis 3f	bird
bos bovis 3c	ox
candidus adj	bright; white; clear
canis canis 3c	dog
cervix cervicis 3f	neck
-cumbo 3 -cubui -cubitum	fall upon; lean on
denique adv	finally
dens dentis 3m	tooth
edo edere/esse edi esum	eat
fera 1f	wild animal
figo 3 fixi fixum	fix; pierce
flavus adj	yellow; golden
frons frontis 3f	forehead
fruges frugum 3fpl	fruits; crops
grates/gratias ago 3 etc	thank
gurges gurgitis 3m	deep water
guttur gutturis 3n	throat
horreo 2 /horresco 3 horrui	shudder (at); bristle
iacto 1	throw about
inanis adj	empty; vain
induo 3 indui indutum	put on
insidior 1dep (+dat)	ambush
lac lactis 3n	milk
lectus 2m	bed; couch
lingua 1f	tongue; language
lupus 2m	wolf
lustro 1	go around; go over
mel mellis 3n	honey

minister ministri 2m	servant
miseror 1dep/misereor 2dep	pity
narro 1	tell; narrate
patefacio 3 -feci -factum	open up
postulo 1	demand
praeceps praecipitis adj	headlong; steep
ramus 2m	branch
sata 2npl	crops
semen seminis 3n	seed
solacium 2n	comfort
sponte adv	of one's own accord
superus adj (superi 2mpl)	above (the gods)
tamquam	like, as if
umbra 1f	shadow; ghost
vadum 2n	shallow water; sea
velox velocis adj	fast
venor 1dep	hunt
vestigium 2n	footprint; trace
volvo 3 volvi volutum	roll (trans)

Word List 17 (Passages 111 - 120)

absurdus adj	stupid, senseless
acerbus adj	bitter
afficio 3 -feci -fectum	affect; afflict
admodum adv	very
aeneus adj	bronze
anulus 2m	ring
beatus adj	happy; rich
caupo cauponis 3m	innkeeper
cognatus 2m	relative
concilium 2n	council
conclave conclavis 3n	room
convalesco 3 convalui	get better
deterrimus adj	worst; worthless
diffido 3semi-dep diffisus sum	distrust; have no hope
digitus 2m	finger
dimidium 2n	half

176

dissimulo 1	pretend ... not
epulor 1dep	feast
erga (+acc)	towards
familiaris familiaris 3m	friend; servant
gemma 1f	jewel
humanus adj	civilised
ibidem adv	in the same place
improviso adv	unexpectedly
insidiae 1fpl	ambush
interimo 3 interemi interemptum	kill
intereo -ire -ii -itum	die
interitus 4m	death
lassitudo lassitudinis 3f	tiredness
maleficium 2n	crime
metior 4dep mensus sum	measure
more (abl of *mos*)	in the manner of
nummus 2m	coin
[diem] obeo -ire -ii -itum	die
odor odoris 3m	smell
pastor pastoris 3m	shepherd
prandium 2n	lunch
proelior 1dep	fight
rapax rapacis adj	greedy
sapiens sapientis adj	wise
sollertia 1f	skill; ingenuity
somnium 2n	dream
sordidus adj	dirty; low
stomachus 2m	stomach; anger
suavis adj	smooth
supra (+acc)	above, beyond
tueor 2dep tutus/tuitus sum	watch; protect
vagina 1f	sheath
versor 1dep	am involved in
videlicet adv	namely

Word List 18 (Passages 121 - 130)

ala 1f	wing
calor caloris 3m	heat

celsus adj	high
cognomen cognominis 3n	surname
coluber colubri 2m	snake
condo 3 condidi conditum	bury; hide; found
continuo adv	immediately
conubium 2n	marriage
coram (+abl) (or adv)	in the presence (of)
corona 1f	crown; garland
corusco 1	flash; brandish
fervidus adj	hot
flecto 3 flexi flexum	turn; bend
foedus foederis 3n	treaty
for 1dep fatus sum	speak
foveo 2 fovi fotum	warm; cherish; caress
fragor fragoris 3m	crash
fulvus adj	tawny; yellow
fumo 1	smoke
funus funeris 3n	funeral; death
gelidus adj	cold
gradus 4m	step
humilis adj	low, humble
ictus 4m	blow
imus adj	lowest; bottom of
invitus adj	reluctant
labefacio 3 -feci -factum	weaken
lapis lapidis 3m	stone
limes limitis 3m	boundary
lucus 2m	wood
Manes Manium 3mpl	spirits of the dead
mitis adj	gentle, mild
noceo 2 (+dat)	harm
nutrix nutricis 3f	nurse
pando 3 pandi pansum	spread out; open
partus 4m	birth
penates penatium 3mpl	household gods; house
portus 4m	harbour
procer proceris 3m	chief
profugus 2m	fugitive
proles prolis 3f	offspring

prora 1f	prow; ship
retro adv	back; backwards
sacerdos sacerdotis 3c	priest; priestess
secundus adj	following; favourable
sepulcrum 2n	tomb
serenus adj	clear; bright
sisto 3 stiti statum	stop (trans)
supplex supplicis 3c	suppliant
tingo 3 tinxi tinctum	dye; stain

Word List 19 (Passages 131 - 140)

admitto 3 -misi -missum	let in; commit (crime)
aestimo 1	value; regard
angulus 2m	corner
assiduus adj	continuous, persistent
cito adv	quickly
clementia 1f	clemency
cogito 1	think
commodus adj	suitable; useful
contingo 3 -tigi -tactum	touch; happen
defero -ferre -tuli -latum	inform on
desidero 1	desire; miss
disciplina 1f	training
ebrius adj	drunk
emo 3 emi emptum	buy
expedio 4 (expedit impers)	free; prepare (be useful)
ex[s]tinguo 3 -tinxi -tinctum	put out
frequentia 1f	crowd
ideo adv	for this reason
imbuo 3 imbui imbutum	immerse; imbue
immolo 1	sacrifice
inritus/irritus adj	vain, futile
intermitto 3 -misi -missum	interrupt; cease
iocus 2m	joke
item adv	in the same way
licentia 1f	freedom; licence
loco 1	place

179

manumitto 3 -misi -missum	free (a slave)
mensis mensis 3m	month
mulier mulieris 3f	woman
mundus 2m	world; universe
opinor 1dep	think
peregrinatio peregrinationis 3f	travels
perspicuus adj	clear; evident
planus adj	level; clear
prosum prodesse profui	am of use
pubesco 3 pubui	mature
quilibet quaelibet quodlibet	any[one] at all
quin etiam	furthermore
reprehendo 3 -prehendi -prehensum	rebuke
rupes rupis 3f	rock; cliff
sanus adj	healthy; sane
silex silicis 3f	flint; hard rock
summa 1f	sum; main point
suppedito 1	supply
taeter taetra taetrum adj	horrible
ultro adv	of one's own accord
vado 3	go
verbero 1	beat
vitium 2n	vice; fault
voluptas voluptatis 3f	pleasure

Word List 20 (Passages 141 - 150)

aer aeris 3m	air
agnus 2m	lamb
amarities 5f	bitterness
apis apis 3f	bee
baculum 2n	stick
calidus adj	hot
canus adj/cani mpl	grey/grey hair
careo 2	lack
cesso 1	am idle
coerceo 2	confine; check
cor cordis 3n	heart